Transmission
Speaking & Listening

Volume 4

Edited by Sharon Kivland, Jaspar Joseph-Lester and Emma Cocker

SITE GALLERY

ISBN 1–899926–66–6

Published by Site Gallery
Edited by Sharon Kivland, Jaspar Joseph-Lester and Emma Cocker
Designed by Ben Weaver and Patrick Ward
Typeset in Bembo, Celeste, Letter Gothic and Univers Condensed
Printed by MacDonald / SSN
Distributed by Cornerhouse

A catalogue record of this book is available from The British Library

Site Gallery
1 Brown Street
Sheffield S1 2BS
United Kingdom
www.sitegallery.org

Cornerhouse Distribution
70 Oxford Street
Manchester M1 5NH
United Kingdom
www.cornerhouse.org

Sheffield Hallam University
Art & Design Research Centre
Sheffield Hallam University
Sheffield S11 8UZ
United Kingdom
www.shu.ac.uk

Site Gallery

TRANSMISSION: SPEAKING & LISTENING

Preface

The Sheffield School of Art was founded in 1830, and was the basis of what became Sheffield Hallam University. Despite its location in a provincial city, the Fine Art course developed a reputation for subversive and provocative art in performance, installation, video and film, as well as in more traditional mediums. As the contemporary art world gradually aligned itself with emergent technologies, the course did not look so eccentric. It continues to offer a space for young artists – at both undergraduate and postgraduate levels – to develop away from commercial pressures, while insisting on an engagement with the historical and contemporary debates and practices of the production of culture.

Site Gallery is an international centre for contemporary art, offering a changing exhibitions programme of photography, film and video, installation and work using computer-based technology backed up with a comprehensive calendar of conferences, artists' talks, events and short courses. Housed within the organisation is the i-lab, providing a well-resourced production facility for still and moving image making, whose focus is on commissioning new work, providing a base for residencies and offering an open access membership. The development of on-line activities, a bi-annual live art event and off-site projects further its mission to make opportunities for creative work and to present new work to new audiences. The gallery offers a site for connections and confrontations between the artist and the public and a national focus for critical debate surrounding the creative use of the still and moving image.

Showroom Cinema is a four-screen culturally-driven cinema, one of the largest independent cinemas in the country. It forms part of the Sheffield Media & Exhibition Centre, which also includes the Showroom Bar and Café and the Workstation, a cultural business centre.

This publication has come out of a lecture series, formerly open only to students, in which artists, and occasionally speakers from other disciplines, present a discourse on their practices. The collaboration between the three institutions has allowed a wider public, and thus has opened debate. The title of the series, *Transmission: Speaking & Listening*, indicates our intention. Although the lectures are absent from this book, the speakers retain their presence in other ways: through short introductory texts to their practice, works conceived for the pages, and as those taking part in a dialogue with others. Commissioned essays frame the discussions, taking up what it means to speak, to listen, and to construct meaning or work in the interstice between the two.

Contents

Editors' Introduction

The first semester's lectures in the series, *Transmission: Speaking & Listening* take up the theme of 'provenance'. Provenance generally means the place of origin, yet it takes on rather more complex meanings in relation to art and art objects, and the market or value systems that contain them, as Steve Edwards' essay so elegantly demonstrates. Provenance may refer to the relation between an art object and its exhibition venue, its juxtaposition with other objects, other artists, with collections, critics and catalogue essays, as well as to other matters of lineage or traceability. For the connoisseur, the search for an art object's provenance serves as a guarantee of the object's authenticity. It may also be considered in terms of a cross-referential indexical system, mapping relations between people, objects and their place in the world. Indeed, in *Transmission: Speaking & Listening*, provenance may be traced. Gabriel Gbadamosi's lecture, written and performed in response to 'provenance' is reproduced here.

The second series of lectures addresses the reading of works of art, when works of art are produced as texts or incorporate text within them. This might imply that they are designed to be read and if they are read, then they might be supposed to deliver up meaning or lend themselves to unambiguous interpretation, unlike other works of art. Yet works that are letters or have letters (in many forms) are just as elusive as other works, seldom spelling out their message in any literal way. Letters are pictures, and pictures too may be deciphered as textual systems, but there are no pre-existing sets of equivalences that will guarantee complete comprehension. Inscription, the act of writing or engraving, is a process forming subjective identities; writer and reader are bound in a relation in which interpretation, inexact or partial, has formal effects. The lectures were followed by a symposium, and edited versions of the presentations of Pavel Büchler, Sally O'Reilly and Jane Rendell, followed by a discussion, take the place retrospectively of an essay framing the theme.

Provenance

Provenance: or Pig Bones & Saints' Bones

Gabriel Gbadamosi

At primary school, I woke up in the middle of narrating a play and didn't know where I was, the lights were shining in my eyes, the big audience was there in the dark and I kept talking, but I didn't know if it was the beginning of the story or the end. At fifteen, I did it again to socialize myself – when I couldn't do *Hawaii Five-O* on my own any more, Columbo or Kojak, whatever was on television Friday nights back in the 70s – I joined the Old Vic Youth Theatre in London.

The Old Vic was once run by Laurence Olivier who started the National Theatre there. Back in the 70s, the Inner London Educational Authority (ILEA) used it to run a youth theatre that put on *Romeo & Juliet,* the O-Level set text. It was a charmed circle: ILEA pays for a youth theatre to put on the play, ILEA pays to bus in the school kids doing it for their exams, ILEA decides it's *Romeo & Juliet* for and by the kids. The two thousand seats are packed out, every night. I'm playing Capulet, Juliet's dad.

I'd never seen two thousand teenage girls giggle. It's infectious. It looked like someone booked in only girls' schools in that spirit of segregating boys and girls in their education. On the first night, it's true, we had a Romeo who was a bit effete, so when he says 'Oh, Juliet, thy beauty hath made me effeminate', they all fall about laughing. You don't mind, especially if you think you should have been Romeo, and who among the boys in the cast wasn't jealous? But once two thousand girls have got their teeth into you – in your pretension, with your stockings on, with their teachers there, pretending it's Shakespeare and not a play about teenage sex – they're not going to let you go, they're going to shake you to death.

It's pandemonium now in the wings, people don't want to go on stage, they have to be pushed on, so they end up looking like they've just been pushed on and they're not ready to be there. But remember now, I'm the girl's dad. I have sisters who are teenagers, and I see how my dad reacts to them growing up and going out with boys – the unreasonable, jealous, anxious, violent, irrational possessiveness of our dad. So I come out and they giggle at me in my stockings, but that's the scene in which I get to beat up and drag Juliet by her hair across the room and tell them that I know why they're giggling. I know it's nervous, and that right now I am that man that someone has to kill before they can be free. The silence that falls while I glare at Mrs. Capulet, daring her to say anything, the silence of two thousand teenage girls, is a terrible thing. It's embarrassingly public; it's complicit in thousands of fetid domestic sexual struggles between mothers and fathers and daughters. It's powerful; but I'm the one with the power, I'm the monster, I'm the one that's going to be killed, sometime, down along the line, by this audience, as I can feel it, hear it, assessing how to stop me, in the end, devouring the maiden.

Of course, that's not how it ends. Juliet's death, that's almost accidental. And I'm not to blame. But I remember thinking, theatre will be the death of me. Unless I can do a quick change and say, after all, that's not me, that was a mask, I've just taken it off and had a shower, and your daughters, no harm done, eh?

Rather, let me introduce myself as a writer. I began writing in primary school. We had this *Daily Diary* we had to do. I was writing in school about what happened at home, and then speaking at home about what was happening through this writing I was doing at school. Writing gave me a voice (I'm the fourth child of six children) to speak and be heard, to understand, to interpret. Whenever one of my older brothers beat me up, I couldn't make my strangled, bloated, beaten up sobs stop long enough to get out my version of what had happened so he could be taken back to the orphanage, or the dump, the deepmost pits of hell, wherever they'd got him from, and dropped. So what better than pen and paper? Or, later, when it's my father who threatens the stable, rational, hopeful order of the universe, how better to reflect that than through the parlour games of writing for theatre?

That's, in one sense, the provenance of my work – in my teens and in primary school – taking provenance, that is, as biography, as my formation, my psycho-social DNA. There's the implication, of course, that by taking two points and plotting between them, it could also give you an indication of where I'm going. But I don't see my life as a straight line. I could hit both those points on a time-line with a parabola; or perhaps with a circle I could go on living them forever. Like that of a lot of poets, my work happens in a day-dreamy chronological reverse, remembering or re-collecting experience in the past. So instead of asking, What's the Provenance of my work?, I decided to hunt around, do a straw poll of curators, art historians, clever people I know – with jobs – and ask them, What's Provenance? Well, says one, it's the history of the ownership of moveable objects. People don't, for example, speak of the provenance of a building as they do of paintings, say, or furniture. It's about stuff you've got to track. If it moves, if it's got legs, it's got provenance.

It can move very fast, says another, because it's 95% market manipulation. You've got a Raphael copy, Madonna of the Pinks worth, what, a couple of hundred thousand? Someone says, no, that's... the real thing, writes it up, gets it hung on the wall of the National Gallery and the John Paul Getty Museum goes after it for £35 million. Its provenance – its history as the real painting – is entirely modern and very expensive. It's basically that critic and that gallery saying it is what they say it is, and it's worth it. But other people agree with them, and although the £22 million finally paid has been called 'a record price for a fake', it's not unlikely the Duke of Northumberland might have been sitting all this time on a Raphael without needing to pin it down in his tax bill.

But how do you prove it? I'm wondering. How do you prove something's the real thing? Taste? Well, you can have the lucky find, the skilled eye and judgement of experts and connoisseurs – a Leonardo da Vinci left in the leaves of an unopened book that was overlooked – but nothing quite beats an empirical history of who owned an object, approved it and passed it down to its present owners and value. The market wants to know that what it buys – authenticity and value – is stable and won't collapse. Provenance is a price support operation. Keep your eye on the money.

But why does my OED say the word only comes into English from the French in the late eighteenth century? Ah, says a third, there might be two reasons for that. In the eighteenth century, people went on the Grand Tour to Europe looking for the remains of classical culture – Greece and Rome – and brought home fakes mocked up in some back alley off the Grand Canal. How good was their French? Did they have Italian? Those modern languages, not Latin or Greek. Orphans of classical Empire, they got ripped off trying to buy the material culture of their dreams. You'd want to know, was it really something Caesar touched? Or it might be the Revolutionary sales. Oh, the Revolutionary sales? Yes. Remember, in 1793 and '94, there were important auctions by the State in Paris of goods confiscated from the Monarchy and Aristocracy. The English aristocracy did a roaring trade through agents in Paris buying up the Royal collections. Which is why a great deal of seventeenth- and eighteenth-century French loot has been held in English collections. If it came from the Queen, Marie-Antoinette, it had a collectable provenant, or Provenance: it was royal furniture. On which count, Provenance came into being between the guillotine and the gavel. Going, going, gone?

Cut, says the lady who's been knitting a frown quietly in the corner. All this about the money is nonsense. Go to a museum, think about it. Once a museum's got something valuable in its collection it's not going to be sold. It doesn't have a price. You're looking at the history of an object, what it tells us about where, when, why, how it was made, what it meant and how it comes down to us.

Why do I like hanging around museums? Perhaps I like this idea of provenance released from history – the history of its place in the market – into being the story of an object under glass. But I can't help worrying, in these smash and grab days, how firmly a museum gets to hold onto an object like that, frozen in place. So what about Baghdad? I ask. The looted Museum of Antiquities? Aren't those things flooding the marketplace? They can't be sold openly. They have no provenance, they could be fake or stolen; you're on your own with the Black Market.

But lots of things have been bought and sold, I come back, that the Nazis looted, and we haven't got to the bottom of what the Soviets took. After a while isn't all theft absolved by history? Forgotten? Finders keepers..?

It's true we live with fakes, she says, with breaks in the history of objects. Fractures along the rim of things we know existed but can't completely be sure have re-emerged. Something lost or stolen can be found. Stealing is ingrained in human history; for objects it becomes part of the story. You can unearth something lost that's been buried. Sometimes that's how it gets preserved. And besides, in time the fakes can become obvious. A fake from the 20s won't look the same as one from the 50s. A clue, some element of style, invisible to people at the time, does after a while become apparent. And some fakes are really good. They can be interesting in themselves. For example, when not only the objects are faked but how they then get fake provenances to go with them. Such and such a collection was known to have such and such an object which was lost. It was known to have existed, is unlikely to meet itself coming back from the auctioneers, is credible enough to pass muster – and all subsequent buyers want to back up its story.

Now that's where it gets interesting. When you get buy in. If you do that with an art object, that's fraud. But in my line it's fiction. I love fakes. Fake etymologies, fake provenance, making it up. I'm on the side of the forgers. I love lying to power. Though it felt odd lying to the Queen when I met her. I suppose I didn't feel she had any power. 'What were you doing in West Africa?' Oh, studying mortuary rituals. Where did that come from? Actually I was strolling around with some travelling players in Nigeria, and I suppose I didn't want her to think of me as a sturdy beggar. Or perhaps that is what I was doing. My father – a Nigerian – had just died. I went and got some money to go and study theatre in Nigeria, and perhaps to mourn him, certainly to walk his land, and, if I think about it, to figure out how, finally, to bury him... but I digress.

I was speaking of fragility and fraudulence in the provenance of things – in relation to my writing and my work in the theatre. It's my job, as I see it, to convince you that this... pig's bone... is more than that. Theatre is unlike Fine Art in that respect; it relies on a willing suspension of disbelief, of the evidence of your own eyes. You can see it's a pig's bone, boiled in France, smuggled through customs only this morning. I'm not hiding it. Now pardon my French, but if I say to you, would you kindly think of this as the relic of a saint, what skin is it off your nose? if in the end, you, too, get to make an imaginative leap and come to think of it as holy? It was a life.

To give you time, I'm going to show you some slides of some crosses. This first one is Spanish, made around 1060 for the King of Castille. It's ivory. The outline of the cross you see is how it's displayed. The original cross would have been ivory. You can see a rationale for the shape of the cross in the human figure. And ivory is bone.

This one is Byzantine, around 950AD. It's in Germany, in Limburg-an-der-Lahn, near the Rhine. The wood you can see is a fragment of the True Cross. It's the kind of thing that prompted Erasmus to wonder how many forests could be assembled from fragments of the True Cross. But that would be one hell of a wood to take a walk in, wouldn't it? While we're on the subject, there have been thirteen recorded foreskins of the infant Christ in Italy alone. Sometimes, really, less is more. But there's also the miracle of the many.

This last one is in the Aachen treasury, where the Holy Roman Emperors were crowned and Charlemagne was buried. It belonged to Otto III, from about 1000AD, as his processional cross. The cameo you can see is a contemporary portrait of the Roman Emperor Augustus, so it's a thousand years earlier, from about the time of Christ. Apparently Otto saw himself as having a dual Provenance, from Roman Empire and Christianity, in some sense descended from both of them. This is the back of it, with the Corpus engraved.

And here's a painted Malevich cross from 1915. Upside down.

I, too, have a dual Provenance, or descent. As a poet – the person behind both the diarist and the playwright – I would locate the provenance of my work in my relation to words, to language. What language? Well, English, of course. But the Provenance is a bit more complicated than that. There's my father from West Africa, so I grew up in a house with people speaking Yoruba, a tonal language, in which in order to speak you have to sing, and you can't be tone deaf when you listen. And then there's my mum, Irish from rough old Limerick – Stab City, because that's how they talk, in-out with a quick jab and you have to be quick to catch it. Beneath her English ran an underground tributary that is the Irish language – not just the brogue, which I couldn't hear and my friends could, but direct grammatical transpositions and figures of speech from the Irish that made her speaking so unlike what you heard out in the street. Under my mother's tongue, then, I found poetry. And in my father's, music.

From these different parental relations to English – my mother's brogue which I couldn't hear, my father's Yoruba which I couldn't understand – there's not only a dual Provenance for my English but also a break, a discontinuity. Most people, to listen to me, wouldn't think of me as Irish or, to look at me, immediately understand that it was my mother who taught me how to speak. So let me focus, as something that might interest you – you might even be wondering about it – on my relation to my father's culture in West Africa. I don't know anything about it. He wouldn't tell me. Except that I know off my own bat most people get to be familiar with it through Voodoo. It's not unusual that I know nothing. It's what happens with secret societies controlled by a gerontocracy. The old guys keep you in your place by not letting you in on the secret. You have to steal it, like fire.

Dad, I'd say, why didn't you teach me Yoruba? Because I didn't think you'd need it here. I was gob-smacked. How could he cut me off like that? Or again. Dad, why didn't you tell me any of this stuff I'm finding out about Yoruba culture? Because you'd go and put it in a book and everyone would know it was me who told you. Dad, how can you be a Christian and be a devil-worshipper at the same time? Go ask your mother. And she being a fierce Catholic, I didn't.

For a while I was outraged at what I took to be the outright theft of my inheritance. I decided I'd go out and get my patrimony without him. I would source myself from him whether he liked it or not. Until I found myself one day, on stage, speaking with my father's voice... So I backed off and thought about it. What does it mean to have this multiple Provenance? I felt suddenly lost.

Have you ever wondered what it means to meet the Devil at the crossroads? That Robert Johnson thing, in Voodoo from Haiti, up through jazz in New Orleans and into the blues? Where the blues guitarist goes down to the crossroads to make his Faustian pact with the Devil to play the blues as no man should? The crossroads is the unknown, you don't know where the paths lead – indeterminacy, choice, unhinging the fixed order of things, of the moral universe. If you see the Devil as a transgressor, who breaks and crosses boundaries, you can see from the Malevich that's what a cross enacts.

That's what it's like for me, with my Irish catholicity, and my Yoruba culture, in which Eshu, Elegba – or in Haiti, Papa-Labas – is god of the crossroads, of chance, of interpretation and danger, the devil, the deceiver.

Let me remind you, I started this talk with one or two auto-biographical fragments attempting to source a Provenance for my work as an artist in theatre and writing. I then fictionalised my enquiry into the nature of Provenance with various art historians and curators. Always bearing in mind that the unreliable narrator is not new to fiction, I found my way to breaks, discontinuities, thefts, fragments and forgeries. My unannounced guide in all of this is a very English version of Eshu, the Pardoner in Chaucer's *Canterbury Tales*, who freely admits that he's hawking pardons and absolutions from Rome, along with pigs' bones he leaves it to the sinners to imagine a Provenance for as holy relics. But I, he says, 'must think / Upon some honest thing while that I drink'.

I too embrace forgery as an imaginative leap across boundaries and breaks, because I need to. The boiled bones of Provenance for my work are something I invent. So let me play you a short clip from a play I made called *Eshu's Faust* which took place in Jesus College Chapel in Cambridge at the crossroads of a cruciform nave and transept. A rather transgressive place to conjure the Devil, a thousand year old English chapel. But I did it with the support of the Christians in the college who felt it challenged and awoke the sacred nature of the space. The secular intellectuals, who usually had nothing to do with this residual adjunct to their academic institution, were outraged at the blasphemy and changed the college constitution to block any further outrage getting past them into their Chapel. Too late. Eshu was then doubly inscribed as having passed beyond them into the constitution and into the walls, into the history of the place which has seen play performances since at least the seventeenth century. I always hated the way those colleges had 'private' signs up across their enclosed courtyards and immaculate lawns. It looked like you'd be treading on strange, tribal territory to try to get in. I was definitely going to trespass there. And Eshu is the great enabler. The Eshu dancer you saw was Koffi Koko, a Beninois Voudun dancer, with Peter Badejo, a Yoruba dancer based here in Britain, as Faust. On the first night we discovered that Koffi had been dancing barefoot over broken glass, and Peter fell and badly bruised his arm on the stone floor. So the next night we sacrificed a white cockerel in secret and bled it into the stone, because you cannot go anywhere without sacrificing to Eshu at the crossroads.

Many people were magnetized by the vulnerable, broken-looking body of Koffi as a version of the crucified Christ, who as you saw there retreated through the rood screen back towards the altar. I had by that time become conscious of wanting to practise an aesthetic of trespass – as is hardly avoidable for a black writer approaching the English stage, it has such a history without you. That trespass is also back over history – not only the history of the Chapel but also of English theatre, in this case Christopher Marlowe's *Doctor Faustus* on which *Eshu's Faust* is a deliberate act of trespass. The trespass amounted in my mind to a revisionist challenge to a history that excluded me, to origins and identities – a Provenance – I absolutely intended to steal.

Gabriel Gbadamosi

Gabriel Gbadamosi is a poet, playwright and critic. He was a Judith E. Wilson Fellow for creative writing at Cambridge University and a Wingate Scholar researching performance in Africa. He has worked extensively in Europe, Africa, the Middle-East and the Caribbean as a writer and lecturer. His plays include *Eshu's Faust* (Cambridge), *Hotel Orpheus* (Schaubuehne, Berlin) and *The Long, Hot Summer of '76* (BBC), which won the first Richard Imison Award. He recently collaborated with artists Conroy/Sanderson on *Sun-shine, Moonshine* (London: Artwords Press). Gbadamosi is the current Chair of writernet and lives in London.

Contributors   *John Clark, Emma Cocker, Lesley Sanderson, Tracey Welch*
Chair   *Sharon Kivland*

TW *What is true and what are lies? You say things which are obvious, but how much was of it was true?*

GG They are truthful lies. Let's take Chaucer's 'The Pardoner', he's saying here are some pigs' bones and he's having a good time drinking. There he is thinking, and he's trying to think honestly, as he says, people have needs, they do bad things in their lives and maybe this pig's bone isn't Saint Peter's thigh bone but if the guy needs it to be then maybe...

Audience *Do you always lie?*

GG To power, always.

Audience *Are truth and lies not just a matter of opinion?*

GG My talk has been more than about truth and lies. I was asked to look into the mirror of myself, my origins, my identity, my practice and convert that into truths that I can market to you. I attempted to go through that process to show you that in my case it would be a bit tricky. I substituted some of the breaks, the fractures and the downright fabrications that are necessary for me to operate as a person, as an artist, to show you how I go about it. I was as honest as I possibly could be. Or rather, I was as useful as I could possibly be on this subject.

Audience *I was interested in your writing at school, the provenance of your work. You seemed to use it as a way having your own voice, telling your own stories. How important is this voice to you?*

GG I think of that diary now as a direct form of confessional writing. It originated as a reflective conversation about family relationships in which I wanted to encourage my parents to take my brothers to the garbage dump. There was certainly a purpose in this writing and that in itself is a point of origin for the making of my work. It also asks what is 'authentic'. I sincerely did want them to take my brothers to the dump. Is there a traceable link between that and the voice or voices that I adopt now? There is a link but to trace it you have to negotiate breaks, changes of mind even. One of the things that circumscribe a political practice in work is that you're not able to be inconsistent. Inconsistency, contradiction, fiction, these things are enormously important for our work to represent ourselves and our world accurately or usefully.

Audience *I am interested in what you said about fiction, about breaks and discontinuities as a bridging of boundaries and your thoughts about the discontinuity of your background in regard to your parents' provenance. I wonder about fiction as a creative process for healing discontinuities.*

GG It was very wounding to be told by my father that he didn't teach me Yoruba because he didn't think I would need it here. So in that sense healing would be right. But actually what the guy is doing is right, he's doing what he's supposed to do, he's being a good Yoruba daddy. He's telling me that he's cutting me off now: 'You swim in this water.' That's what I'm supposed to do, so there was no wound. The educational process, the way culture reproduces itself is by breaks, by cuts. I don't propose the logic of the talk as one of healing or wounds but rather a description, dispassionately as I could, of what happens when I don't have my father's experience. I don't have his language, I don't have his history, I'm cut off from it. I have to figure out my connections to the world. Not everything is a wound you should rub salt into. You can conceive of these experiences in different ways, needing different action.

Audience *Do you see transgression in relation to authenticity as a political gesture within a cultural practice?*

GG I'm not sure I understand the question but I'm going to speak to it anyway. I did dig out all these lovely slides of crosses and I thought that would gently ease people over into seeing the cross as a continuous image in Western Christian culture. Then I began to edge in these little fractures. Imagine a formal place, a structure, x marks the spot, the crossroads. What is the transaction there? Is it so clear to us? Can we in the same place and at the same time have another thing happening, can we put a devil on that cross? Can they co-exist? This is a proposition, in my experience as an artist, about what I do and how I live my life. There is always a sense of an order but exactly where I believe something, I radically disbelieve it as soon as I say I believe. That is mine and Kierkegaard's experience of being sentient. Now your question is about the location of authenticity and transgression as a political practice?

Audience *I could have said the dislocation is at the point when you can say something is located and you may as well say it is dislocated.*

GG Yes, it's the cross, it's a shoulder joint, it's linked and at the same time it's also a rupture.

LS *I want to understand your use of Christian references in your writing. Am I to think that this is where you can be most subversive or do you return to Christian imagery and ideas for some other reason?*

GG I'm a good old-fashioned Catholic boy, can't you see? In our house we had Anglicanism, Catholicism, Yoruba culture and radical secular liberal atheism, all crammed into our heads at the same time. I was a greater pagan than I was a Catholic because Irish Catholics are really pagan. I thought about pigs' bones and saints' bones for this talk; I love Chaucer's Pardoner hawking around these fake bones. I love that image and I love that person, he's my patron saint. So I came to Catholicism, to crosses. It was visual, for visual people.

LS *You do in other writing too. Do you come to Christianity because of its stories?*

GG I was fed from my mum's knee on Christian stories. And I count myself lucky that I was born into a family of devil worshippers at the same time as God worshippers. It's an interesting proposition. Eshu is both male and female. Such images as there are of Eshu are twinned figures, man and woman, usually wrapped in cowrie shells and unpleasant things like maggots.

Audience *Could you say more about the relation of writing that is written to be read and writing written to be heard? Are you conscious that what you are saying is going to be written down and are you going to rewrite that?*

GG Yes. I decided to write this talk rather than write an outline on a single sheet of paper, which is my normal practice. There were a number of reasons that I should do it this way. One is that I should make a piece of work for you, so you can see me doing it in the spirit of openness and transparency. Much of the way that I function as a writer is in the clarity of the functioning of my reading and my writing. This is how I write. Can you hear it, can you see it? You will hear the shifts in tone, you will hear the flaws in my syntax, you'll hear how I can't quite pronounce 'discontinuity'. This is my process, it's flawed but I wanted you to see me performing. I also wanted to make sure (because there certainly exists within race politics the idea that black is oral) that as you saw me here, black artist that I am, you saw that I functioned in another way than the oral performance of the poet. I love writing for a speaking voice because, in my view, lots of English poetry since the 60s has increasingly abstracted itself from the speaking voice. If that sounds Wordsworthian or romantic, then I'm sorry, but whereas these poems may work in clever and sophisticated ways on the page, they are not for a real speaking person. Performance poetry, black performance poetry, seems to be the inverse of that. People say that there's nothing on the page, it's all about the performance. So the performativity of the word seems to be important and should be abstracted from racial cultural politics. It is about enabling people to use the voice, as well as writing, to communicate, persuade and change things.

EC   *There were glitches in the presentation when the relations between the text as a written text and the text as a spoken text became more apparent. The crossroads between a literary and a spoken culture appeared at those moments.*

GG   One of the things you can do as a writer is the enacting of that thing which goes with thought, the breaks, the stops and it's always good to be broken just in case you are going on and it's nonsense. Breaks are also self-critical. They're new starts, new chances, new possibilities of getting it right.

Audience   *What is the difference between provenance in art, and in literature or theatre? I was interested in the way you spoke about the provenance of the image in fiction and I want you to take up the notion of plagiarism.*

GG   Bad writers plagiarise, good ones steal. People not only steal, they also fake. I don't know how I could make it more explicit, because it was the subject of my talk. If one thinks of a writer, say, Daniel Defoe, what a forger, he's always lying, if he doesn't lie he's not got his back covered. You know the way in TV dramas you love those figures and criminals that the flying squad always picks up as informers. That character is always interesting – you really want that person grabbed by the neck, giving you any answer, always faking, always thinking. That is always fascinating in fiction about the fake, the forging of things. I don't know what the challenge might be for visual artists if you are producing works into an order in which lying is policed.

EC   *Site Gallery held a conference that took as its premise the idea that the artist is the chief con artist of the world. As an artist you are asking the audience to take a leap of faith in believing what you do has inherent value.*

GG   Plato excluded poets and artists from his perfect republic, essentially because when there is an order, a good political structure, a well-functioning society, copies are not necessary. Artists who want to fake it, the copy of a copy, this is just too much, we have to exclude them. It's not the way that I think about the world. I think more is more.

SK   *What does that mean?*

GG   More copies is more copies. More versions is more versions. Pluralism is my standard.

SK   *I want to ask you about the difference between generations of immigrants. When you return to the old country, the country that is not yours and has never been yours, what do you find there, what do you know about it or about yourself? I know a family of second-generation Italians from the south; when they go back, they're called the English. They're never going to be Sicilians.*

GG I never went to Nigeria or Ireland until I was grown-up. I remember landing in Dublin, getting off the plane, being taken out onto the tarmac and interviewed for the television. I was organizing an Irish Arts Festival in London and I had to publicize it in Ireland. Off I go to the pub and then, a bit drunk, to a press conference. I really had a rough time in that press conference. One question: 'So wouldn't you say these black men sleep with white women as a form of revenge for slavery?' I got through it and went to another pub, a big pub in the centre of Dublin, and I'm finally sitting there trying to get my breath back and onto the television news comes Gbadamosi. There he is. It is my first day in Ireland, I'm trying to be anonymous, and there I am on the television news that night. Of course it's going to be tough and of course I'm not going to be able to get the measure of my size in this place. One feels a giant in Nigeria because one has so much more money. You can turn bigger wheels, so you feel more of a giant. I'm sure that's what lots of Americans feel when they go back to the old country. My experience isn't very different from that of any immigrant who goes back to a country with a bigger status and in the next generation.

SK *You were going back as a guest. What about those people who go back because they are lost here and are looking for homeland?*

GG There's a good Irish story about that. In the old days there was a great court and one of the characters out hunting in merry old fairy Ireland gets taken up by the Fairy Queen into her bower under the green hill. After a couple of weeks he says, 'I have to be going home now'. She says, 'Don't go.' 'I'll be back,' he says, 'I'm just going to visit.' 'Okay, but don't dismount from your horse,' she says. So he goes home and sees that everything he's known, all his old friends have all passed away because time passes differently in fairy land. When he tries to touch the ground he ages in seconds, turns to dust and the sea wind blows him away. That's the story of the immigrant who can't return. You can't go back, there is no way back. I always stay on my horse wherever I go.

SK *Something came up today about what kind of relation might be possible between art and writing, how writing might be part of an art practice? Now you are a writer firmly on the side of literature and I see you hanging around with artists, so could you tell us more about that?*

GG Theatre draws on many artforms, music, dance, architecture and painting. As a teenager, in my search to learn Englishness, I fell in with a school of English painters from the Slade, all taught by William Coldstream – it used to be called the Euston Road School. They would go on painting holidays to the south of France, and while they went during the day to all their various sites to paint, I would look after the house. I got the hang of the table talk of artists and I got the hang of talking to them about work. I've never let go of that relationship to visual culture. More generally, what are the potentials for a relationship? Think of illuminated books from the fourteenth century, there has always been a relationship between visual arts practice and the written word. Most of the students I've met here have a relationship with theory, which usually comes through words and those words are echoing in their heads. There is always writing around, through, and under. I'm very interested in the relation between the printed word and art.

JC *What's so special about artists writing and a writer writing? What happens when a writer makes art? When an artist writes or when an artist makes art there is an inseparability of form and the content. One is founded on the process of the other. You made a break in the talk when you showed the slides of the crosses, and it is as if the cross represents the break in form, which is part of the presentation – in fact, the relation between art and writing.*

GG There were many breaks in the talk; that was just one. My way of talking is allusive, leaves you your space, your fantasy. You don't want to come to a talk after a hard day's work and sit in a half snore before you go out for the evening. I want you to relax. That's one of the uses of breaks. Another is to stop myself waffling on. Another is to renew. The process of breaking and renewing is also an invitation to dialogue in your thinking as well, which I only referred to once when I wondered if you were wondering about my relationship to being African, because many English people wonder about that. The form of the talk was painstakingly crafted so it would continue to give you stuff after you leave here. It may be useful to you and if it is, I'm pleased.

Christopher Landoni
Love Triangle
2004
Mahogany, formica, enamel paint
244 x 325 cm

Erratum

THIS PAGE IS INTENTIONALLY BLANK

Blank Page

Pavel Büchler

I would like to warn you that, unlike the previous speakers, I am not going to give a paper; this is going to be a presentation. There is a difference, not least a semantic one. These days we artists give papers; I remember a time when we used to use paper to make drawings. We presented those drawings in galleries. Now, in conferences, we confer our papers onto our audiences. To give a paper implies presentation, like giving a present. We present somebody with something which we believe that person or those people would like to have – a drawing or a text, perhaps. But what do you give to people, yourselves, who have just been presented so generously with so much?

To make a presentation means to make something present. We make presentations to call up something, bring it into the present, manifest its existence. Or at least, by the combined powers of imagination and photography, we conjure up a phantom presence: a projection on a screen. There was a time before PowerPoint presentations when we used to have slides, when pictures on the screen did not silently cut one to the next but every time you pressed the forward button there was a short gap, like a word space, and the reassuring mechanical noise of the moving parts of the slide projector to let you know that the machine was working as intended and the show would shortly resume.

All I am going to give you, for the present, is a blank page. Well, not even that. Here *(opposite)* is picture of a photocopy of the back page of the Association of University Teachers' National Executive ballot papers of 2001. The text, printed prominently in the middle, claims that 'this page is intentionally blank'. Something is not quite right about this. Obviously the page is not blank, let's face it. On the other hand, it is intended to be perceived as blank, surely.

In every act of writing, written communication, anything on a piece of paper (which is not what I'm giving today, but what I'm trying to make present), intentions seem to be mixed from the start. I want to present to you a blank page, but can't leave it just as I was left with it in the trade union booklet, intentionally blank. The true intention of the author of the page, the AUT returning officer, is not to give me any blank pages in my ballot papers, no bare, self-evident blankness. He makes this absolutely clear; there can be no confusion. Just imagine the panic that the paid-up trade union members like myself would feel if we received blank pages. The author anticipates my intention, that of the reader, who wants to get something from the page for his £9.20

not forms and colors

after Joseph Kosuth after Douglas Huebler after Lawrence Weiner ... *Artforum*, Vol. 36, No.3, 1997, p. 16

a month union fees. Now, what can I get from a blank page? Nothing, presumably. Can I get any more from one that offers me a proposition that is true only if it is false? The third intention is the intention of the page itself. It wants to be blank. That's what the text articulates, against the author's intentions, and what I must recover, as the author intended, so that from the page, overruled by the tautology of the sentence, I get something that I may only get from a blank page that speaks for itself. The words 'this page is intentionally blank' complement and contradict what I see as much as what I read. Paradoxically, the page would be blank only if it was not meant to be so. What it says is not what it wants to say and what it shows is not what it wants to show.

Ever since about 1750 we have been told that works of art are particularly good at having their own intention, a quality that makes the work simultaneously invite and resist interpretation by permitting improbable readings despite of what is written or shown, seen or read. The intention of the work is what the author and the reader have to negotiate to make present what is already 'there'– and at the same time respect that what is there is never fully uncoverable.

What is there when there seems to be nothing? Not forms or colours, to be sure. This piece of paper, in front of us on the screen now *(see opposite)* seems much like the intentionally blank page. It is an art work, albeit a modest one. At the bottom of the page you read 'after Joseph Kosuth, after Douglas Huebler, after Lawrence Weiner.., Artforum, Vol. 36, No. 3, 1997, page 16', the work's title as well as an acknowledgement of its pedigree and provenance. It was commissioned in 2003 by the curator Lars Bang Larsen for a project that invited the audience to participate by photocopying the artists' contributions, to bring out what was there. As they waited by the photocopier to see what comes out after all the writing in art magazines, the discoveries of the giants of conceptual art, and after my own feeble efforts, it may have crossed their minds that what was there was already present.

This, finally, is an intentionally not a blank page from my forthcoming book, *Conversation Guide* – here it is, as blank a page as you can ever get. *(See overleaf)*

Pavel Büchler is an artist, teacher and occasional writer on art, film and political culture. A founder of the Cambridge Darkroom Gallery and former Head of Fine Art at the Glasgow School of Art, he is currently Research Professor in Art and Design at Manchester Metropolitan University. Recent publications include *Conversation Pieces* (i3, 2003) and *Saving the Image: Art after Film*, co-edited with Tanya Leighton. (CCA, 2003). He is participating in the Istanbul Biennale, September 2005.

THIS PAGE IS INTENTIONALLY BLANK

AUT National Executive Ballot, 2001

Transmission: Speaking & Listening
Volume 4
Edited by Sharon Kivland, Jaspar Joseph-Lester, and Emma Cocker

Erratum pp. 180-4

SITE GALLERY 2005

Christopher Landoni

Christopher Landoni was the winner of the EASTwork commission at EAST International in 2003, Norwich Art Gallery, which resulted in the presentation of an outdoor work at EAST International 2004. Other recent exhibitions include 'There and Back Again', Program, London, a solo show at Museum 52, London, and 'Expander', The Royal Academy, London. Landoni began his lecture by showing slides, selected at random from an archive he described as sharing the characteristics of 'impossible places, narrative landscapes', speaking of the narrative drive of painting. These were flicked through, so the image was held for a moment, creating a curious sense of loss and memory. He described his relation to images as one of greed, and the implication of oral satisfaction and pleasure arose as a linking theme throughout his talk, insisting on an avoidance of ethics, morals, philosophy in his pursuit of pleasure. Landoni read his own translation of a short story by Dino Buzzati, 'Master of the Universal Judgement', which tells of the terrible seduction of images (and beauty, trembling on the edge of terror), of possession and haunting. He made an identification with the romantic idea of magic, the possibility of entering another world where linear time no longer operates, and his own strategy of concealment that ensures that the viewer has to slow down. This was demonstrated in a sculpture, which he described as being 'an individual component from a drawing', and recent paintings with seductive, fantastic scenes, depicted in black paint on saturated black monochrome surfaces. The fantastic, escapist quality of his work is indeterminate, and Landoni suggested that the intricate images, drawn from diverse sources such as fairy tales, the gothic novel, the history of art and the organic imagery of the natural world should elude the viewer, who is forced into a delicate negotiation with space if there is to be any yield of meaning. Landoni addressed the engagement of the spectator in artifice and illusion, in what he called the 'borderline'.

Contributors   Carole Baugh, Emma Cocker, David Gomersall, Horatio Eastwood, Jaspar Joseph-Lester, Alice Maude-Roxby
Chair   Sharon Kivland

SK   *You talked about the way the paintings slow down viewing and while you were saying that, you were flicking through the slides at quite an incredible rate and suddenly I was just looking for the X where you had selected the image. On first encounter with your work it's invisible, and yet it's not invisible because it's a great black mass taking up space. One isn't reflected back. It absorbs the viewer and then very gradually what is there starts to emerge, and one starts to drift across the image physically, not just in a mental state but actually moving across to catch it, engaging in some kind of macabre dance in order to call the image into being. Would you say something more about the construction of a poetic space of approach where one sees something that's nothing and then the nothing becomes a very particular something.*

CL   The point of flicking through all those was to show that there is just so much available. We know how many thousand of images there are but somehow it is still a surprise. I called it 'the bottomless pit of art history,' but actually it isn't bottomless, it's quite defined: from this point then to now. The black on black, first, it's important that you slow down; second, I wanted to make these as night drawings, I wanted these worlds to exist in nighttime so the way of making a night landscape was to paint black on black. I wanted people to slow down and have a personal experience, to engage with the image. Third, and most importantly, I didn't want the image to be immediately obvious; I wanted only certain parts of the painting to be seen at any given point so the entirety of the painting was only formed in one's mind.

DG   *I am intrigued by the sense of mystery and illusion that's created because you do have to look through these impossible landscapes. In the story that you read there were the shades of another world existing at the same time as our usual reality, in the way the landscapes of Bosch simultaneously exist. Your work is illusionary in the way it unfolds as you walk through it. What are your motivations for putting these disparate parts of art history together — is that part of creating a mystery, a fantasy?*

CL   No. If you want really good apples you go to... where would you get good apples?

SK   *Cézanne.*

CL   Okay, you go to Cézanne. If you want really good salami you go to... if I want really good drawings, I'll have a look at etchings by great masters. There are a few people I am interested in and there are certain paintings that have a certain quality. My generation has been largely quite an escapist one, and that's reflected in the work.

EC   *There was a similarity in the way that you showed the slides in relation to your paintings. In both, you seem simultaneously to be revealing and concealing what your references are. How important do you think it is that people can identify what the sources are, or to whom you are referring?*

CL   In *Let Them Eat Cake*, it is important that it is the horsemen of apocalypse that are being trampled because it opens another narrative, Dürer was talking about anarchy and rebellion, so there are times that specific references are important, in opening another narrative rather than the obvious one that is the façade.

EC   *The idea of provenance is interesting and it was highlighted in the introduction in relation to the notion of connoisseurship that the work demands a certain kind of knowledge of the history of painting. Is there an expectation that in order to get the most from viewing the work you need to be aware of that history?*

CL   Art is elitist. I don't for a minute believe that you can make art like the Daily Mail. There is a time and place for everything. There is enough for everybody in one of my works. They are made beautifully – that's intentional – they are crafted objects and so anybody can relate to them on some level. But it's like anything, the more you know, the more you can find. It isn't only connoisseurship.

EC   *In the work with the skeleton and the linoleum plinth, there are quite different types of provenance. People who are in the know would be able to find references to painting and then there's this lesser provenance of the lino and the 50s tower block. There are different stories and different kinds of lineages there.*

AM-R   *I was interested in the story you read of the image of a pencil doing a drawing like an apparition of a pencil doing a drawing and at that moment I also thought back to the slides you showed, and my realisation as you were clicking through them that these are the slides that you've used to make the piece, not just as reference but as an actual tool, projecting slides to paint them.*

CL   I project them, and then I draw them.

AM-R   *You didn't talk much about the physicality of making your paintings. Is it intentional that you don't want us to know?*

CL   Yeah, I'm quite shady about that. I think that it's not important. It's like my Mum said to me, the difference of making a good risotto or a bad risotto, you can make a perfectly edible risotto by adding the wine, putting in the stock and you just mix it a couple of times and you leave it and it's perfectly edible, but a really good risotto would be a risotto that you stir for a very long time. So as long as my intention is to make a beautiful work, it doesn't really matter how I get there. In fact, it really doesn't matter if I do it at all; at the moment I have people helping me. What do you think?

AM-R   *For me, there was an excitement in suddenly thinking that these are the slides you've used, marked with a red cross.*

CL   No, it was just a bag of slides that I had in the studio.

HE   *So you are taking another narrative, building up all these things that aren't well-known but to a person who does know about them, they may sound a bit obvious. They can make all these connections but then you are hiding it in their relations to each other. The links aren't clear and then you are hiding the narratives with the black medium. There are obviously messages but what are they?*

CL   What's the message that I'm trying to convey? I don't know that I have a message to convey. Are you asking me why I make art?

HE   *I suppose so.*

CL   I think it's a worthwhile activity.

HG   *What makes you come to these images? Do you love the images or do you love the stories and what they conjure up in a person's mind?*

CL I'm not sure, to be honest.

HE *How would you like an audience to react to them? What sort of thoughts would you like to be evoked?*

CL I speak for myself. If I trace back my practice, before I went to college, I would make tons of work during the course of the day, lots of throw-away stuff. I used to make quite a lot of video. It was all badly-made stuff; a lot of energy went into it. I was quite hyperactive and I came to a point where I really need to slow down. I wanted to make something really well and so I started to make glass etchings, again imaginary places essentially, from various architectural sources. I read about buildings that were going to be built but were never built and then I would make an image of this building. But I found that I was making rather sterile work, so the black drawings brought both those ways of making work together. I had all of art history, any image that I could possibly want, so it was about opening things up for me. With an infinite source of images to choose from and the patience to actually sit down, what I wanted to make were beautiful objects, in which people could lose themselves. They are quite selfish as works because they give you something but they also push you away.

SK *It was a terrible question to ask, Horatio.*

HE *Why?*

SK *It's a question that artists dread being asked.*

HE *I did try and phrase it in a polite way.*

SK *It's still the question to which one never knows the answer.*

CL It changes with each piece of work, don't you think?

HE *It wasn't so much about the meaning, but rather why you are doing it at all.*

CL Because I really enjoy it.

HE *It was more just picking up on all these recognisable references, like Dürer.*

CL I'll tell you why I'm interested in those people if you like, if that's what you are asking me?

HE *It's just that they already convey a message and so what do you hope to convey by using them?*

CL The message is something quite different. You are talking to me about ownership and originality and I'm not really sure what that mounts up to.

HE *No. It's the wrong word. It's just they convey something.*

CL I don't believe for a minute that art needs to have these expectations like messages and political issues and ideas. It's enough for people to look at something and enjoy it and not to think about the mortgage they have to pay. As long as they have a nice time when they go to the gallery, then I am happy.

HG *Then you've answered my question.*

SK *We feel guilty that we should enjoy ourselves. What we don't see on the slides is the beauty of your paintings, they are like velvet and satin, really luscious. Indeed, they are like a good risotto. (I think we both come from cultures where food is quite important).*

JJ-L *It's interesting these questions have come up, as these aren't always questions that always arise in this setting. There is something obviously that sparks that question in relation to your practice.*

CL It's something I ask myself everyday and there are days that I say, yes I am happy with what I'm doing and then I can spend months wondering why the fuck am I doing this but I think that is common to most artists.

JJ-L *What really struck me, what made me want to ask similar questions, was the obsession in the work. There is a compulsive obsession that comes through in the way you make things. I think that was partly why Alice was asking how and why you make something and in fact, why you didn't perhaps talk about that because it seems to be such a big part of your work. The slides are fascinating because it seems like you are just obsessed with images. It begs the question about motivation.*

CL Escapism has got something to do with it on a personal level and also on a sociological level. My generation has been one of the most nihilistic and escapist generations that there has been. That has rubbed off on me and the work reflects that.

JJ-L *There is a thing about death in the work, in the kind of excess.*

CL Yes there is, but that's something else though.

SK *When we think of escapism we think about a delightful place but in escaping into one of your paintings it is not a particularly lovely place. It's a place where terrible things are happening, but in your paintings we can take pleasure in the things we are not allowed to do in the world because we would be put in prison. It's an escapism into the seething Id of the unconscious where all the things one dreams, and then tries to forget, are allowed.*

CL There is this incredible façade, so beautiful that it draws you in and then as you investigate, as you get closer, it isn't all so beautiful or rewarding or warm. I was thrown by the question because my work has changed since and I have been asking myself why is it that I am making this stuff and why I am dealing with these things and why I have been so interested in death.

Audience *You spoke about the masculine and feminine and it seems to be a big thing in your work – the beautiful flowers feminizing the subject, trying to make it more palatable.*

CL I use them as an aesthetic device. Nature that has been incredibly sexualized and made into an object of desire and at the same time belittled like pornography. Nature is an incredibly powerful thing. In many of my works, the backgrounds are made out of carnivorous plants, which seem beautiful and serene things but actually have a power of their own, so yes, there is a duality there.

CB *I suspect that part of what we look for when we look at a painting, is to see how the artist sees. There was the part in the story when the protagonist is sitting in the park talking to the old man and he asks if he is saying that two hundred years ago these strange creatures roamed this earth and he replied that he simply could see within the commonplace, he depicted what he saw and how he saw the world was a revelation. That seems to me to be an explanation of what the process of painting is about. So you have a look at a Van Gogh and you think, I'm looking at this because it's within this tradition and then you go to Holland and then in a way, you see through the eyes of the artist. To me, they all tell the same story. It's like seeing the same things. I don't find the speed of the slides different to the speed that occurs in the slowing down of the implacable surface of the painting. What is most striking about painting, is that it appears both precipitous in terms of making it and it defies control. So when you are watching it you are watching it with this speed. When you tell the story what came out of it was to do with the fabulous and the fantastic and the magical but then I also sensed that there was a moment of another kind of vision.*

CL I could have spent the last couple of months writing an essay on provenance but I didn't want to do that. I wanted to keep it more conversational and open and honest. I'm sure you can make work about what you don't know but work largely reflects what one sees and what is around. Art history and all these slides, the story, they are just tools. I use these to recreate a feeling or attention – that's what I I'm interested in and on which I reflect.

At the moment of this book going to print, we learnt of the tragic and untimely death of Christopher Landoni. All deaths, all losses, mark us forever, just as we are marked by our meetings with extraordinary people. Christopher Landoni will be greatly missed and we are honoured to have met him and encountered his work.

In Memoriam, then: Christopher Landoni, born 16th February 1972, died 29th June 2005.

Goshka Macuga
Kabinett der Abstrakten (detail)
2004

Goshka Macuga

Goshka Macuga's work explores the boundaries and categories that define exhibition structures. In collapsing the distinctions that divide artist, curator and collector Macuga 'provides a total environment for the exhibition of other people's work, in which their work becomes her work and her work theirs. This expansive approach to art practice has lead to a number of ambitious installations in this country and abroad.

Macuga discussed how much of her time is spent collecting work that she likes. Instead of collaborating with contemporary artists, Macuga chooses what she feels is most relevant: 'I am interested in personalities, people I work with, people I like, the friends of people I like... I shop for things.' In *Picture Room* at the Gasworks Gallery (2002) Macuga recreated a room in the Sir John Soane Museum. In place of Soane's collection of ancient artefacts, Macuga filled the cupboards and shelves with a selection of objects and works of art from contemporary artists. This broad range of paintings, sculptures, drawings and objects blurred the provenance of individual works. Not only was their authorship uncertain but their place of origin, and consequently their object status, was seen to disrupt any singular or determining classification. In her one person show *Kabinett der Abstraction* at the Bloomberg Space (2003) Macuga drew on the diagrams, teaching methods, writing and art of Malevich. The concept of shifting roles was again central to the thinking and realization of the project, which included works by Malevich, cabinets made by expert craftsmen, book collections from selected individuals, a suit worn by a Russian dog that flew into space, an abstract painting by Warhol and small pieces of sculpture made by artist friends.

Contributors   *Emma Cocker, Horatio Eastwood, Jeanine Griffin, Tom Newell, Nick Stewart*
Chair   *Jaspar Joseph-Lester*

Audience   *How do you think your work differs from that of other curators?*

GM   That's an interesting question because there are several courses on which you can do an MA in curating. They don't have a long history, and lots of curators come with interesting ideas of creating exhibitions and there isn't that much difference between their work and mine. You can go back to exhibitions that you would attach to Duchamp – I think that the title of one of them was *1,200 Bags of Coal* – working with the space, with the collection of work shown at the exhibition. The tradition of curators trying to be artists and *vice versa* is difficult to define. Obviously I fit within this category, but I don't feel there is a need to make a distinction between curators and artists. Do you think that the roles of artists and curators should be clear? What should be the boundary?

Audience   *There are boundaries, but it is interesting to stretch them.*

GM   Many artists break the boundaries. Many people work in areas that are not structured in such a way that you would limit them.

JJ-L   *The figures you are interested in, people like Sir John Soane, Malevich and Rodchenko, were also interested in blurring those distinctions.*

GM   Yes, definitely. A practice based on going to the studio, work produced in the studio and not going beyond, that would be boring, especially living in London and having access to all this information and being involved in dialogue with other people. The exchange of ideas with artists or people who do other interesting things, is something that I value. My interest is in people who also have a diverse character.

JJ-L   *It's a fairly traditional idea that artists have a range of interests and pursuits, isn't it?*

GM   When you read biographies of artists, you discover that while there is the work, there is also another story that you are not familiar with, but which supports the work. When I first read about the early practice of Andy Warhol, his design of shop displays, I was enthusiastic because when I arrived in London, I also worked in window dressing, and in Poland I studied Exhibition Design. Everyone has interests that influence and inform their work.

JG   *I am interested that you said that when someone agrees to be part of your framing device they lose the ability to have a say in how the context of that is structured. If you are working within a gallery system that seems quite perverse. Do you think you have a privileged position as an artist-curator?*

GM   It's purely practical, because if you work with fifty artists with two weeks for the installation and if each artist said how they should hang their work, it would never happen. I rarely get involved with collaborations. That is hell because it becomes a discussion about what everybody means by collaborating and the practicality of putting on an exhibition becomes the last thing. It's egos brushing against each other, trying to negotiate things that are very obvious. It is in some way privileged, but it's more about getting stuff done. There is a tension in having something accomplished, and negotiating with artists causes problems and delays. *(Laughs)* Somebody said that my work is an illustration of pseudo-communism, when everybody is supposed to be equal but at the end of the day I rule. This was very funny and appropriate.

NS   *Is it a critique of other curators? Is there idealism in your practice about art and what art might be?*

GM   There is a part of me that has an idealistic approach, a vision of what art or what the community of artists should be. At the same time there is a conflict. Living and working in London has many positive aspects; you have access to a lot of information and an amazing contact with other artists. But there is great competition. I think of myself as someone who has an idealistic approach to art, yet this is not quite how things are. There is a nostalgic idea about what I imagined art was going to be, before I became an artist.

TN *I'm interested in the artist as curator, such as Mike Kelley's recent project* The Uncanny. *Do you think that traditional curators, who aren't seen as artists, are going to have re-think the way they work, becoming more creative to keep up with people like you?*

GM Recent curating reflects the relation that artists have with the white cube gallery. The showing of work in neutral spaces goes back to the 1930s. Alfred Barr, curator for the Museum of Modern Art in New York, displayed work in neutral spaces with white walls. At the same time, Alexander Dorner made his Atmosphere Rooms, quite opposite to minimal exhibition space. There are periods in which things come and go. Many exhibitions now are environments that frame the works, which has significant importance because it influences the way we read them. This particular attitude is relevant to how we live in a world that never really allows us this neutral space. We are bombarded with things from the outside and rarely have space to ourselves. Perhaps one would idealistically imagine that artists go into the studio and produces work that is neutral, just for them. Recent attempts at certain exhibitions that question the space for the art work or where the art work lives have been valid attempts. It might be a question of fashion or a particular interest of particular curators or artists.

EC *You spoke about the collection of books that people have as individuals, how this is an indication of where they are coming from in their art. How does this translate in terms of your curatorial approach? It seems that the works in the exhibitions are personal to you. Is there an analogy between the works that you might have in the exhibition and the bookcase or your personal libraries? It's like a story of your own provenance.*

GM Yes, the works that I choose or the books that I choose are the works or the books that I would like to have. It's simple, straightforward and personal. I have always had a real passion for books. Coming from Eastern Europe, where there were problems in buying books that you would want to read because some of them were not published or translated there, you would look in the bookshops if this book had come out yet. It's important that I'm exercising this ability or imaging that I might have things that I would have not had before, thinking of myself as a collector. Often you come across people who have collections that focus on different things. I have recently worked for a year in a collection of books that are mainly art books. I have been paid to update the library of art books, so I have access to the most amazing books that I would never have otherwise found because they were out of print. You want to have it or it influences your work, or you could borrow it and have it in one of your exhibitions for four weeks. You don't really have it because you don't live in the exhibition space, but you have it because it's part of your work. The choices are personal in terms of the objects, and in terms of the artists or the collectors that I work with.

EC   *Is it the degree of subjectivity that sets it up as an artistic practice rather than what could be understood as a museum practice?*

GM   Certainly it's not a didactic practice, so maybe that's the difference. I am often asked that question but I don't think about it much. I don't try to blur the boundaries between the curatorial and the personal artistic practice. If they overlap, it's more interesting, it creates more tension in the work, both for me and for people who view it.

JJ-L   *This is also interesting in relation to the artists you work with, because one assumes you have a lot of support from artists for your projects. How do you gain that trust, that support from artists?*

GM   It's a personal thing, from living in England and having a supportive community, like a replacement family. I did a residency in Taiwan for three months: I wanted to do a project with Taiwanese artists, and it was hell because I don't speak Mandarin. I had to reassure them that what I do is significant and many thought that it was only significant to me and they hated the idea of curators. So you would have ten hours negotiation with the translator on the phone with them saying they didn't want to take part, and me trying to reassure them that it was significant or interesting for them to take the risk and give me a chance. I became friends with some of them, and we are still friends now. It's negotiating the positions really, that allows me to have the support of people who find it interesting.

JJ-L   *Do they find it useful to see their work in a different context?*

GM   I don't know. *(Laughs)* I'm sure that they do, but they probably have certain prejudices as well. If my exhibition is successful, does it mean that my success is their success? My second show using this formula was in 1999, a project in Cubitt Gallery. I was working with my partner; we created an installation that looked like a mountain, with special effects of light, we called it *A Mountain and a Valley*, and we asked friends to give us work that they didn't want any more, reject works that people wanted to get rid of from their studios. It was quite funny because then we displayed the work and it looked engaging and interesting and then the artists came and the whole dynamic of the private view was around the objects, everyone was walking from one thing to another and trying to find the narrative and the relation between them. But they also were re-valuing the objects. Depending on the context that you give to work, the work can have a different life and different value. Perhaps it's quite satisfying for the artist when it does happen, when the work does start having life, when an artist who doesn't show their work anymore is put in the context of more contemporary artists. There are great possibilities in what can happen in the situation.

HE   *I am interested in artists who control the whole environment as they build and design it themselves, such as Mariko Mori's* Dream Temple *from the 'Apocalypse' exhibition, where you are completely submerged in this artist's vision. How important do you feel is this idea of artists building their own exhibition environment as opposed to using an already existing space?*

GM   It's the essence of working with installation, that the installation becomes a layer within the gallery...

HE   *I would differentiate between the idea of an installation that is made to be in a gallery, as opposed to these environments which, in theory, could go anywhere.*

GM   It's a problem with relating to installation. I sometimes refer to my work as 'display'. I feel more comfortable with that. But that's another term that people have certain attitudes towards. Obviously it's important for me to create these environments. Perhaps Mariko Mori and I are linked by timelessness, as her work is about an imaginary future and my work tries to escape time, in that it has certain references from the past but then brings it to the future. Maybe it works in a similar way for the viewer. The atmosphere of the spaces or the exhibitions that I try to create is something that I'm familiar with, from my past or where I come from, where you would look at things and you would try to understand why these things are together and you would never find the answer but you would be satisfied with contemplation and an attempt to work something out. I'm trying to recreate a moment where people can stop and think how these things came together, how they interact with each other. Obviously the atmosphere comes with a personal way in how I bring things together.

JJ-L   *I'm struck with this in relation to the idea of these installation spaces as being something that encompasses both art and collections of objects, and how those two pursuits have different value systems. In the show at Gasworks, and at the Soane Museum, there were bits and bobs that could have been bought at a second-hand shop, that might not a have a value at all, alongside major artists' contemporary work. Is that relationship important?*

GM   The bits and bobs are actually by artists. I just chose particular things that look like bits and bobs because I like them. I often use works that don't particularly represent peoples' practice. When I did one of the first shows, *Cave*, at Sali Gia Gallery, creating a cave using brown paper to look like rock, people gave me work that was supposed to be very precious. One of the artists, who used to work with embroidery, was struggling at that time to justify his position as an artist, and he gave me work with which he was experimenting in the studio, a lamp made of paper that no-one would have ever assumed was his because he was doing elaborate embroideries. I like going to car boot sales. I have a collection of bits and bobs at home that I love and I would like to find a space to show it in my work. But it has to be the right moment and situation. The selection of works is significant to my personal taste.

JJ-L *I also love bits and bobs, but the thing that's interesting for me is that the status of those things is transformed, as having seen your work in these spaces you immediately identify those recognisable works, and then you look down at the shelves and you see theses books, and you wonder whether they should or shouldn't be there. It seems to be the value of these art objects that lends value to these other objects.*

GM I enjoy working out how things relate to each other, why one thing should be next to another. My work reflects that excitement about nonsensical juxtapositions.

JJ-L *Earlier today we were discussing Duchamp's urinal, how that first came into circulation through a photograph, very cunningly taken with a painting in the background, supposedly to lend it value as a work of art seen in the right context, and it seemed to remind me of the idea of the early ready-mades.*

GM The works of other artists are ready-mades for me. You could compare it to making sculpture of objects that already have a certain meaning. These works have a particular meaning, and a significant sort of importance to the people who have made them. In placing them together, as whole piece, you could relate that to the tradition of ready-mades, but it is more complex.

EC *In later work it seemed that you were using objects in a different way. I was interested in the references to Byron. It is as if the objects are lending value to the stories – you seem to be using objects in a completely different way.*

GM This is a new experiment for me, making work without borrowing the works. It is a transitional period; I want to have a break and find a way of replacing the original objects with something else, like this imaginary collection of objects. Over the last four years I realise that I haven't got any time outside of these management situations where I have to do a show. I have to make lots of studio visits and I find amazing stuff in peoples' studios and then I take it to the gallery, and these projects can take up to a year or two. I haven't got any mind space to play with things in a straightforward way; setting them together and allowing myself to fail, and then doing something again. Using props, things that are imaginary objects that could be other peoples' work, allows me more space and time to play. The moment of creativity that in the installation of an exhibition would be when I install the work within the space, has a longer period in the studio. It's not a question of life and death, when if I don't manage to do it right now, then I will fail. The table, the portrait of Byron was exactly that attempt, not borrowing real things from Byron's museum but trying to make things that could be there.

EC *That did bring up a question of authenticity. It made me doubt whether the works that were in the previous exhibitions were authentic as well. There was a really nice relationship between the two pieces. It introduced a sense of doubt in my mind that I thought was quite playful.*

GM Playful is the right word to use in this situation because that's what I am allowing myself to do. My future projects will further try to get away from that formal attempt to be consistent within the work, and having to always use other people's work. There are ways around it. So that's what I would like to do in the next few years, occasionally going back to this shopping for art works exercise and putting everything together, but not until 2006 I think! *(Laughs)*

Elizabeth Price

Elizabeth Price's practice incorporates diverse mediums and strategies, including collaboration. A consistent characteristic of her methods is that work is produced over many years, shaped incrementally by ongoing activity and tasks. This suggestion of retrospective and prospective narrative is evidenced in projects in which the artist's actions are intended to continue indefinitely. These include *Boulder*, a large sphere of brown packing tape; *Hearse attending...* an ongoing series of photographs in which hearses wait outside contemporary art venues; and *Trophy*, a silver competition trophy that is engraved with the details of each show it features in. Her work has been shown widely including a major solo exhibition at the Jerwood Space, London in 2004. Price teaches at Goldsmiths College and is currently Research Fellow at the London Metropolitan University

Price articulated a rich conceptual framework, providing an expanded definition of the potential meanings of 'provenance.' Laying particular emphasis on the function of provenance to secure the value and meaning of a work of art, Price explored the way in which certain art practices since the avant-garde have seemed to problematize this. However, although it is accepted that art's value is contested and volatile, the provocative categorical disorder suggested by this, tends to be shored up by processes of connoisseurship and institutional endorsement. This problem is represented through the reflexivity of conceptual art, where these strange politics are both disclosed and amplified. Price asserted that the provenance of any contemporary art object is the narrative of a process of production through and about the politics of patronage and power. Against this framework, Price described processes of her practice in which conceptual models and approaches are established and then disturbed, mutated or overruled. The photographs of hearses waiting outside galleries prompts confusion between symbolic and literal affects, especially when over time each of the featured galleries closes; *Boulder* transforms a rational methodology into a ridiculous and meaningless task through an excess of dogged persistence; and issues of authorship are explored as found texts, instructions and assertions as accepted by the artist as a script or premise for making work.

Contributors *Jaspar Joseph-Lester, Tom Newell*
Chair *Emma Cocker*

EC *You referred to cartoons and a deadpan performative quality. What is the role of humour in your work?*

EP I didn't speak about that so much because I wanted to talk about provenance, but it is characteristic of my work. The stories that unfold have a sense of pathos or failure about them, as in the black humour of the hearse visiting the gallery, and even the unexpected narratives arise from that (it been associated with the closure of some of the galleries). That amuses me. The trophy, with a list of my exhibitions inscribed on it, is my own CV. The trophy is a symbol of success, so to award oneself a trophy is clearly an absurd vanity. I try to keep it completely deadpan; I'm not winking at people, to say 'this is funny', I present my work with a poker face, as though they were straight-forward, serious historical documents.

EC *With the reinterpretation of the text, there were elements that seemed to have a humorous content: your choice of particular individuals to take the role of sixteen-year old boys, for example, in your project* Small Gold Medal.[1] *In terms of a viewer or a reader coming to the work, how much do they need to know already about these individuals?*

EP In inviting these six artists to collaborate with me in re-enacting Chalmers' will I was presenting them with a challenge. I maintained Chalmers' intended exclusion of girls, because I did not wish to euphemise it. The challenge I offered to the 'boys' was to see how they would deal with their inherited privilege. The choice of artists was based on this challenge, and also on the specified age. When I asked those six artists I didn't tell them that I was asking them to be boys, but there was mischief in it. Some of them never noticed.

EC *When one reads the book, it becomes quite apparent who in the group was taking it seriously and who was taking it with an element of light-heartedness or mischief.*

EP Yes, for example, Matthew Thompson found a schoolboy of under sixteen years called Matthew Thompson in the borough to write it on his behalf. He dealt with my challenge by reiterating it. The schoolboy was asked to talk more about the competition and so dramatizes the event.

Audience *I am interested in the progression of your work, which from its start has a period of time over which it develops and becomes something else. How important is it to give the work a space for surprise elements?*

EP Yes, that's important, especially for the later works, which are more complicated, formally and conceptually. The best starting point for wanting to make a work is something about which you are confused or don't know about. I don't think it is useful for me to go through that process in angst-ridden isolation – it is more sensible for that to be public and declared. The works take a long time but they unfold publicly and they are often collaborations. You can't do everything by yourself and sometimes you need people to work with you. I'm becoming increasingly confident about allowing things to become resolved over longer periods of time. I make blunders, and I make lots of stuff that in the end isn't relevant, but there's a reward in the sense of the enquiry not being stifled by the need to resolve it too soon. For many of the projects, it's not entirely in my hands what happens, so I have to be prepared to be surprised.

EC   *This takes up on ideas from previous discussions in this series; there is a pattern, as arguments have been repeated and illuminated from different points of view. There was talk about the role of pause or breaks in work. There was a discussion about how important the pause is as a space to reflect, to renew energy and as a time to invite dialogue. Is this true of the episodic way that you work?*

EP   Each episode has the potential to change the work. The new projects are much more orchestrated. So the pause is important to allow each category a resonance. The next episode realigns it. The works are not subsumed by the logic of their process; there is something particular about each distinct episode.

EC   *They don't seem to be working towards a point of completion. They are much more works in process, mutating along the way.*

EP   Embarking on something artistically starts from a problem or question. That inevitably leads to a mutation; the things one finds out change one's relation to what one is doing, to the world and to the material. Also changes will happen because of contingent factors: political events, other art, things in the world.

TN   *Could you explain about the categories of work that came from or were inspired by Jenny England's record. Some of them seem to have obvious links, like the United Artists sculpture and the Crystal Gayle picture but the first category seemed slightly more tenuous.*

EP   *This Record belongs to Jenny England* is an emergent project, derived from a copy of a 7 inch record released in 1979, by Crystal Gayle on United Artists records. The sleeve of this copy of the record has been appended with a handwritten text. This reiterates the details of the record; describes when and where it was purchased; and states that it is the property of Jenny England. I have decided to build a collection of art to belong to Jenny England, employing the assertions and tone evident in her text, in an attempt to understand and elucidate the affects of her amendments to the original object. In order to build this collection I have established a series of irrational categories under which to generate work: *Drawings of buildings named after people.* In this way, I'm trying to build a framework that will allow me to generate different kinds of material. The first drawing is a drawing of the shop where the record was bought: Bonds Department store in Norwich. I was interested in the confluence of the different individual actions and intentions that this record documented. I wanted to take all the protagonists of the drama that resulted in this object and find a way to represent and understand them as such. Henry Bond was the person who established the shop where the record was bought. I did a drawing of the shop that bears his name. I was interested in the convention of department stores – they have possessive names like Woolworth's and John Lewis' and this strange notion of authorship is exemplified. I was interested in the actual building, his name was clearly upon the building: Bond's. 'This belongs to Bond', in the way that Jenny England said 'this record belongs to Jenny England'. Bond's was established in 1918 and that building was from the 1930s. What are the accumulative effects of that? The category is expanded with other buildings named after other people. So far they are all dead people. New categories will develop to bridge a relation between those that seem explicitly related to the information on the record and those that are more vaguely connected. I am building a collection of art and there are gaps that need to be filled.

Audience *Do you think the narrative of the works will become linked together?*

EP When I saw the building where Jenny England bought the record, it reminded me of the Chalmers Gallery, which was named after Alexander Chalmers. The gallery was established as a result of his Will, and this made me think of Bond's department store as a memorial. So I did a drawing of the Chalmers Art Gallery to add to this category. It helped me understand the Bond's drawing. I have also done a drawing of a student accommodation building in the University of York named after Seebohm Rowntree; a tower block in Bethnal Green named after Charles Dickens, a 70s low rise block named after Jeremy Bentham and a Dr. Barnardo's building. I do edit, so if it is too self referential, it changes. But the works do rely on each other. Obviously you don't do all your work in one project, you build up a sense of what it is you are trying to articulate, what you think about things. All the works have a role; they rely on each other, in their formation as well as their dissemination though not explicitly.

EC *It's a question of whether works make sense on their own or if they make sense in the context of the artist's wider practice.*

EP Our ability to confidently read an art work is helped by a sense of knowledge of that practice. Any artistic practice is an ongoing enquiry and the works that may get generated, or the essays, are symptoms of that.

Audience *Do you have any foresight of legacy for yourself in terms of your work?*

EP When I say my works are indefinite, I mean they will continue but they are linked to my own mortality. Obviously they won't go on forever. They will go on until I can't do them anymore, and there might be a number of reasons for that. I might stop being an artist.

In the case of the series of hearse photographs, the continuance of the work is linked to the continuance of art galleries, or rather the art world. There might prove to be an infinite number of galleries, because although those my hearse visits seem to close down, other ones open up. It is likely that I will die before the art world does, and so the cessation of the project is actually linked to the artist, rather than the subject. My own biography is there, although not explicitly, but it's ever-present as a logic of the work.

Audience   *Why should a dead person have their intentions carried out? Maybe your work doesn't have to cease; maybe you could write instructions in your will and someone can carry it on? How would you feel about that?*

EP   What interested me about fulfilling the instructions of dead people or missing people is the complicated idea of power or potency implicit. By carrying out other people's instructions, I am presenting an impotent or occluded idea of artistic creativity. In carrying out the will of Alexander Chalmers I am acting under his will. But it is more complicated: it is my will to fulfil his. The people I act on behalf of in these projects are dead or missing, and their legacy is in my hands. That is my presumption at least, albeit unendorsed by any authority or relative. So maybe I just imagine I can inherit and alter these legacies, like Jenny England imagined the record belonged to her. I suppose I am trying to dramatize a sense of artistic activity occurring within and as part of a dense and mysterious world of power and authority. There are also different kinds of power. Chalmers' collection of art is pretty rubbish, and the sum of money he gave was small, he didn't really have that much power. He was mimicking art patrons, like Frick maybe. Even so, his power is certainly different to that of Ajiye Akimbolade, the young man who threw himself off a block of flats in East London after writing 'dead body dial 999' on the back of his jacket. There's something about his lack of power represented in the vicious realism of his text on the back of his jacket, which both provokes and mocks action. As for when I'm dead: I wouldn't want anyone to carry on with *Boulder*, it really isn't that much fun.

EC   *It's like a legacy of penance or punishment.* Boulder *is like the task of Sisyphus.*

EP   It's a bit miserable but it's also fascinating and strange, rather like in cartoons, where normal, everyday physical laws no longer operate. As it gets bigger, it takes longer and requires more effort. The same work seems to produce less and less effect. Indeed each roll of tape added to the sphere diminishes the relative impact of the next and I'm caught in a cycle of diminishing returns. But that would only be depressing if there were a real value of achievement in it getting bigger. In a cartoon you can be run over by a steamroller, and you can pop up again, so there's comedy about it. It's not a penance, but it's not a pleasure either.

Audience *You're dealing with subjects like death that have an extreme poignancy, but the work to me is so dry. What you describe as 'deadpan' creates a coolness in relation to a subject that has emotional content. I'm really confused about my own response. I don't find any comedy and I don't have any access to the humour been discussed either. I can't get access to the political dimensions of the work.*

EP It's very difficult to know how to express the things that you feel very intensely about. If you are furious about something, you might have the idea that the most eloquent way to express that would be to do something that looked like you were furious when you did it. There's certainly some art that looks like that, but often such expression can lose itself in the form. I certainly do feel intensely about the things that I make work about. I remember starting art school in the mid-80s, when people were making huge paintings, slapping on paint, as though they meant it, and I couldn't believe that they could mean it. They looked absurd and slightly comic. Yet at the same time I am wary about the way any force of candour seems to be so hampered by self-conscious knowledge of the forms and etiquette of art. But the art world is like something from an Edith Wharton novel; there are winks and there are nods – and expressionism is rhetoric, so how do you ignore that? I do not think innocence or desire is an excuse. My approach is to reflect this sardonically.

Audience *As men can't bear children, they might try to extend themselves in the future by putting their intentions in their wills. Do you feel detached from that and is that where your sardonic humour comes from? You distance yourself from your own mortality by creating autonomous objects.*

EP Most of the people's instructions that I have fulfilled have been men. It's not an accident. In each case, I am carrying out the will of people who hold different relationships to power. How that makes me think about my own potency is of course a question. The *Jenny England* project is different in many ways, partly because the person who I am speaking on behalf of is a woman. That gives me a different relation to the material. I conceptualize the works produced in this way as epilogues to existing narratives. The two examples I gave when discussing the power of the epilogue to re-write a narrative in retrospect, are interesting in relation to politics of gender. Douglas Sirk was a director of women's movies, which were completely marginalized at the time they were made, although there has been a revision of his work; and Carol Shields, although she won the Booker prize, is marginalized as a miniaturist. In both Sirk's *Imitation of Life*, and Shields' *Unless*, what is at the heart of the narrative is never revealed until the epilogue. What was missed, what was overlooked becomes clear in retrospect. Feminism is still young and there's a long way to go.

Audience *Do you feel that your work can only exist when it's in process. I was interested in the works such as* Boulder. *When the process stops, what happens to the objects?*

EP They just become trophies. Whilst they're in production, there is a sense of possibility. Narratives unfold and they are not concluded and that leaves some kind of space. I think it's there in conceptual art, the pathos of this. At the Manzoni show at the Serpentine Gallery, I saw the atrophied balloon, once full of the artist's breath and thought this isn't the artist's work, this is evidence that the artist's work isn't here, a little memorial showing you where it used to be. Much of Manzoni's work reminds you of this fate. That's where *Boulder* without the idea of its continuance will be.

EC *You didn't talk about the project* Snowballing, *which is an interesting metaphor for the working process in the sense of accumulation needed to keep momentum going. The moment that stops the thing ceases to exist. It collapses.*

EP That was a collaboration with about forty artists in my studio, which was open for a year every Friday afternoon. The artists who contributed made works which accumulated over that time. For example: Fergal Stapleton wrote a novel and he gave me a page every week. At the end of that year the collection it was exhibited as a closed/complete archive and then disassembled entirely at the end of the show.

JJ-L *I am interested in the way that you were critical of your own practice at moments in your talk, saying that you felt it was too reflexive and you used the words 'too neat' or 'too tidy'. Is there an issue then with that work returning and at the same time being uncritical of it?*

EP I'm critical of certain works in that I don't wish to return to working in that way. At the same time they were a way for me to try and understand conventions of exhibiting and what art galleries mean and do. But I'm not really interested in finding more versions of the same work; it seems boring. I'm interested in what they may still generate, and what will continue to unfold. There is still stuff to be understood and learnt, but I don't want all of my time to be used up on it. I want to dedicate most of my time to projects that give me more space.

EC *When we think of an artist's provenance as a record of exhibitions, we forget that there are many things that never materialise.*

EP Editing is important for artists. We don't have endless amounts of time and money so we want to direct our activities as carefully as we can. But it is important to work speculatively. Editing in advance is difficult and can be limiting. Often what you need to know in order to decide whether something is worthwhile, you will only come to know through working with it. Most of the time I do something on a hunch, and then think what it means, which can take a long time. It's important to remember that some stuff will always turn out to be rubbish. It goes in the bin.

1 A book work that observes the Will of Alexander Chalmers, who upon his death in 1927 bequeathed his collection of art and one thousand guineas to Stoke Newington Library. One of the terms of the Will was that six essays on the Art Collection were to be written by boys still at school and not older than sixteen years. (London: Book Works 2001).

Overleaf left:
Elizabeth Price
Hearse attending the Cambridge Darkroom
1998
Colour photograph

Overleaf right:
Elizabeth Price
Hearse attending the 3 Month Gallery
1997
Colour photograph

Preceding pages, left:
Nigel Cooke
Smokestack in the Sun's Eye
2003
Oil on canvas
183 x 244 cm

Preceding pages, right:
Nigel Cooke
Smokestack in the Sun's Eye
Detail

Nigel Cooke

Nigel Cooke's paintings oscillate between extremes; he works on an epic scale but dwells on the minutiae of decay and dissolution, he paints with scientific accuracy while creating scenes that could never exist. Cooke was born in Manchester in 1973, and studied at Nottingham Trent University, Royal College of Art and Goldsmiths College. He is represented by Modern Art, London and Andrea Rosen Gallery, New York. In 2004 Cooke has had solo exhibitions at 'Art Now: Tate Britain' and Andrea Rosen Gallery, New York. Group exhibitions in 2004 included 'Monument to Now', Athens, and 'Sodium and Asphalt', Museo Tamayo Arte Contemporaneo, Mexico City,

Cooke engaged with painting's 'provenance' which, seen through modernist theory (Greenberg, Bell and Fried), was understood to possess meaning as a consequence of one particular history or origin (cave painting). Cooke described how his paintings dealt with a broad visual register that undermined any possibility of an overriding provenance. The relation between unusual and often unsettling visual combinations was shown as key to Cooke's fascination with painting. The 'multi-temporal personality' of his work was also discussed in relation to the viewer's engagement with a mutating visual field. At a distance, Cooke's paintings could be understood to shift between the grand traditions of history, landscape and high modernist abstract painting but close-up the detail revealed an extensive array of contemporary detritus; monkeys defacing the surface with illegible graffiti tags and severed fashion heads strewn amongst burnt out vehicles. This expanding flow of information was seen to relate to the co-existent operation of molecular and super-molecular systems in nature, systems performing actions that are not cultural but reside in the open systems of bio-mechanics.

Contributors   *Emma Cocker, Steve Dutton, Sharon Kivland, Tom Newell, Nick Stewart*
Chair   *Jaspar Joseph-Lester*

SK   *I'm interested in the broken, fragmented, apocalyptic horizon of the painting. The horizon reminds us that we are subject to limits. What is happening in the rest of the painting? Is that where our death lies?*

NC   It is about facing something completely ungenerous in its possibilities. A desire to pacify is absent in my work. There is a termination point that exists when you take away the centre, where your head would naturally be positioned and your eyes would rest peacefully on the picture, exactly where you are confronted with a blank. The horizon is where things begin; I don't think that there is death there. If there is any life, that is where it is, where nothing meets something. The death of the mind you're talking about, is in bringing a desire for the centre of the painting to be full, where it is not rewarded. It is how children make paintings – they do a strip of land along the bottom and the sky along the top, in the way a Zurbarán still-life has a flat foreground and then a back of the box where all the fruit are hanging. That fundamental shape is very straightforward, once it's developed and put in this context it is disturbing because there's nothing there.

Audience *Would you say more about the connotations of the graffiti with the weight of art history?*

NC It started in a painting of a wall from a concentration camp with a small piece of graffiti scrawled on it, 'Don't buy from Jews'. I made that the subject of the painting; a nasty little element that looked innocuous but the painting could not live up to it. It's a way of dealing with the failure of painting to live up to its content. Connotations follow, about defacing your own painting but also the idea of a lost signal, something which you could once read, but now is just a signal, not something you could understand. Its connotations are about the subjective desire to do that, like the young people who do these things in their local environment to communicate. That's exactly what's happening in the painting – one element of my character is stamping itself on another element. These are all dimensions of painting. I have tried to get away from any sociological content, making an issue of an element of subversion that is washed away by time. In the world of paintings, graffiti is often rubbed away and indecipherable. There is a ruined splendour, a romantic lost ideal of affirmation.

SD *You said that high production values used on meaningless images open up a space for thought. Do you mean you can distinguish between a space of thought that happens in painting that is somehow different to any other thoughts that might occur when one thinks?*

NC Surprising collaborations of phraseology and content open up thinking. That's a fact of communication. Comedy is good at doing that – its randomness with an intent and purpose can often make you see things in a new way. For me, it's specifically painting, this thing which so many people are hostile towards on one hand and which on the other, has a global market. The production values are deliberately turned up to the max. It develops out of the bad painting thing, which I went through myself, in the early 90s, a passive/aggressive thing saying painting is dead, but let's do it badly just so that everyone knows we know it's dead. That was an incredibly passive way of dealing with it. What happens if you try painting as well as you can, so excessively that people ask what on earth are you doing, why you spend that long, there are better ways of delivering an image and furthermore, it's all fried chicken boxes and crap, all out of proportion. Things then become critical rather than just affirming.

SD *Are you suggesting that it is a space of reverie?*

NC The idea of communication as straightforward has always been problematic for me, that there is something in the work that you either get or you don't. I have tried to erase that, because I am more interested in what might develop like Chinese whispers amongst the community of people involved in the work. I maintain that the works are not about anything, but they are about that in a forceful way, and that paradox or tautology is a definition of painting.

JJ-L *What is striking about the way you discuss your work is the emphasis you place on painting, as if you are interested in getting to an essence of painting. In saying they are about nothing you seem to be suggesting that they are not concerned with a single history, origin or essence which might stand alone as a trusted conveyor of meaning. When you spoke about provenance, I thought that your notion of competing visual languages, the resistance to the emphasis on linear origins in modernist theory, was precisely where your paintings held their meaning, in a tension that is both spatial and conceptual.*

NC The idea of them being nothing is one of pluralism and circularity and non-linearity, the essence of what these paintings are trying to be. Essence is a difficult conservative term. Maybe the essence of painting isn't something that takes painting away from the world as it used to, but actually reintroduces it as a system like many others.

JJ-L *If you don't know about painting there is a chance that you might be left with nothing. They seem to thrive on the struggle between competing visual histories and languages that emerge from painting as a thing in itself.*

NC That is certainly true, there is a way in which that conversation is pitched at the initiates who know the story. There is another level where people respond in a direct way to the work, the style and the touch, as though it equals value. In terms of the market, people still relate the time spent to value. I have tried to problematize that. Instead of saying why don't you pay me a hundred grand for a painting that took me ten minutes, I say, why don't you buy one which has taken me six months and has really been a difficult thing to do. If you can make that provocative, that will be a more interesting and useful debate about value and utility and expenditure and market forces, and all the rest of it. Once your work has become a commodity, you have to build a debate into its production.

SK *To return to your remarks on mimesis, research on insects that camouflage themselves shows that just as many camouflaged insects are found in the stomachs of birds as those who don't camouflage themselves. In short, in the natural world, camouflage doesn't work and moreover, it causes problems; taking stick insects as an example – if a stick insect looks like a stick to a bird it might not get eaten, but unfortunately it also looks like a stick to another stick insect, so they don't then reproduce, which is another kind of death.*

NC   You are referring to Roger Caillois' essay? It gets worse, they mistake each other for food, which is a dangerous by-product of successful representation. There are other things which they get wrong too. I've seen evidence of phyla camouflaging themselves as autumnal leaves but on spring bushes, as one brown leaf, perfectly like an autumnal leaf but at the wrong time of year. It's the pathological content of nature that fascinates me. It's not that it's not successful – if we had it in a tank with loads of foliage, you wouldn't be able to see it – but once it starts nibbling on its friends and its family, that's not success by anyone's standards. In non-closed systems in science, it is where you are in the system, from where you're observing it. From the perspective of the kid in the classroom with a box full of stick insects, it's incredibly successful; in the jungle feeding on an autumnal leaf is a disaster in for everyone, because not only is it eating the wrong thing, it's going to be spotted by a different kind of predator which may be poisoned by it and it might impact on the ecosystem in different ways. I am interested in where you are in relation to the system and that is what I try to engender in the work. It's a different conversation if you're close, middle-distance, far away, in the presence of one or not.

EC   *The paintings remind me of petrie dishes, where cultures form, so the severed head becomes a culture within the larger structure. In natural systems, there are mechanisms for limiting activity. How do you impose restraint on your practice?*

NC   Most of the time it feels like it's out of control, it's more random and instinctive than it looks. People think they're projected images, that they are collaged on computers, but the truth is I wing it in the studio with the materials and hope that it works out. They have a limited vocabulary of forms in a deliberate attempt to create a system of communication between their elements. While I'm painting, a head might be too big or coloured so that you read it, not in relation to the world, but within itself as a relational thing. It's like a bonsai garden where everything is miniaturised even though it looks vast; a bonsai tree looks like a tree a long way away. My paintings are like that; you don't know where you are in relation to the object. I need to limit the range of things that take place there, so there aren't monkeys and horses or fabulous creatures, it's prosaic things that happen, but in the rendering is where the events take place so it pushes the horror to the sides because it's about how and why it's done.

EC   *And the references to bacteria, to viruses and contagion?*

NC   Painting is full of analogies, Frankenstein's monster, the return of the undead. People like to make analogies with painting and that is my preferred one. Nature has flows of information to change it, then you can look at all systems in that way. Painting is coloured mud on a flat surface but it mutates in unpredictable ways in a predictable framework. That is exactly how organisms behave in the wild. If you think about research, which has moved away from the Newtonian idea of closed systems, into flows of matter and energy through crystallization points, then why not see painting as part of that. Maybe it is the crystallization point that is bizarre in that you have billions of years old pigments and very up to date chemicals mashed together in a material clump, pumped with information by this agency called an artist. It is an odd organism; it relates to different times in perverse ways but nevertheless, if you are invited to see the world on those terms, through information theory – the idea of flow – then why not have that as a crystallisation point, rather than something which is a screen or projection, fantasy space for people's desires about representation?

NS   *The works are like stage sets, as if something might happen in them – what is your relation to performance or theatricality?*

NC   They do look like props and people have made a relation to the work of Samuel Beckett (though I have never particularly related to it), although it's quite obvious with the heads and the pared possibilities of narrative. Rather, it is about having a limited amount of possibilities, but also an endless amount of possibilities, without claim to any energy or agency. The heads are inert; the graffiti is old, nothing has any agency of change, except me.

NS   *There is a sense that something might happen, or has happened, of expectancy.*

NC   That is a product of the things looking like they are rendered inert, by some force either before or after. The point of that is to refer back to the artifice of the painter. These things are mobilized as painting tropes first, content second and that connection engenders possibility, space, time.

JJ-L *There is also a strong relationship between theatre and traditional allegorical painting, like Poussin making models of stage sets to paint from.*

NC   The allegorical landscape is really significant, especially considering Poussin. You are invited to think about how the natural world affects human aspirations, and he constructs a theatrical space to show this, a snake kills a man or flames overwhelm some towers. It is a way of saying you are looking at a grand space, with moments of threat and meaning and possibility. The man with a snake wrapped around him is a harbinger of the vanity of human aspirations. For me, it is the vanity in human aspirations to want to find the snake in the first place. What looks like the end might actually be the start.

Audience *The scenes of your paintings are like a paradise lost, the innocence of the organic world mixed with a crude artificial world, and of course the heads — do you identify with those heads?*

NC Do I identify with them? I think so...

Audience *Why do you put them where they are?*

NC I put them where they look best, that's the most important thing

Audience *You don't look for comfort... for a comfortable place for them?*

NC They don't comfort? I make them look elegant, putting them in the right place, a conventional idea of composition, as if I were using oranges and lemons instead of burnt-out Ferraris and severed heads. The image changes but the thinking is the same, that's how they get placed, by ignoring what they are.

Audience *They always seem to be looking outwards at the viewer — are they not concerned about what is going on behind them?*

NC They look around. The eyes of some are closed, some are open, some look out, some look at other heads, some look at objects. The identification is with being a spectator in the picture. There is a certain thrill in the little face looking back from this vast thing.

JJ-L *They are fairly healthy looking heads, they don't look like they've been around for too long.*

NC They're not necessarily dead either, they could be growing like cabbages. If you went to a different planet, you might get a description of these paintings — there are people that walk around but you don't say there are bodies.

TN *Are the heads portraits of anyone in particular or are they your interpretation?*

NC No. They often change gender and hairstyle, they're taken from fashion magazines, but I change them,

TN *There is no significance in which they are? Do you succumb to the temptation to put your friends in?*

NC I have thought about it.

JJ-L *They wouldn't be your friends for very long.*

NC It depends who they are. What's important is that there is no relation to things outside of the painting

JJ-L *Your interest in Francis Bacon?*

NC Originally it was his studio that I was interested in, making that the subject of the painting. Gradually I became more interested in his work. He uses very limited means and vocabulary to achieve a range of effects, and there is also the idea of artificial production values. He uses bodies as abstract shapes to articulate the painting in classical composition or golden section — if a head needs to be further to the left, then he stretches it. There is no fidelity to integrity and humanity; it's all about painting, a way of seeing things that overrides ethical, moral and personal responsibilities. That is what that I attempt in my work, not as a statement about moral responsibility, but as a function of painting. Bacon was concerned with painting at the expense of everything. His paintings aren't portraits; they are heads like fists, like clumps of flesh. They have a greater presence than a face, without the traits of emotion and personality. There is a sense of an overwhelming obligation through the mechanics of painting.

SD *Why did you feel you needed to do a PhD?*

NC Life was different when I started it, I was in that shed and it seemed like a good idea. Somehow I finished it, I never really thought that I would. During the time I worked on it, my career began to exist, which it didn't before and that changes everything. A PhD is quite a servile thing and I have started to think about writing a book about painting. Now I am on this international treadmill it is great to know that there is some integrity, as well as this show, that art fair.

SK *I am sorry to return to the heads, but if they are dead, then that makes you a serial killer, doesn't it? You are even arranging them decoratively, like serial killers do. But I don't think that they're dead. I think they're alive. Is yours a libertine vision where all is available, all is instructive – but oh, what pleasure lies in destruction?*

NC There is an element of a fantasy of ultimate availability, a 'pornotopia' dimension of detail, which is about ultimate visibility. But they are not that excessive, they are abandoned and available but actually there is nothing, no possibilities, no particular delight. There is nothing profane about it. If I was a serial killer, or Paul McCarthy... if they were his heads, there would be hotdogs in the eye sockets. They are all quite nice, they seem to be talking to each or approaching each other romantically. It is more like gardening than killing.

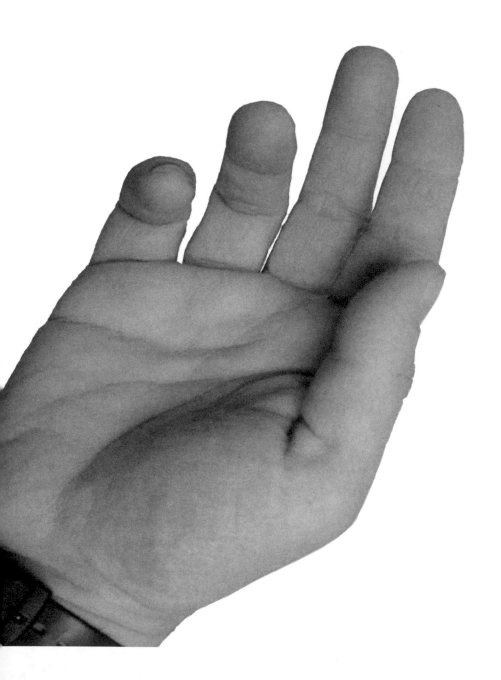

Julian Walker

Julian Walker is an artist and writer working with museums, preserved sites and objects. He has worked with the British Museum, Liverpool Museum, Kettle's Yard, Cambridge and was the first artist-in-residence at the Natural History Museum, London. He is currently working on a cross-disciplinary project with the Royal College of Physicians.

Walker traced a psychology of collection, in which objects act as reflections of identity, discussing how the projection of knowledge elevates objects and surroundings gain meaning from their contents. He explored the relationship between objects, text and the past, examining hierarchies of language and the sense of physical presence residing in objects. Taking up Walter Benjamin's concept of the aura, and its reduction by an environment of mechanical reproduction, Walker suggested that reproductions might act as acolytes for their originals, referring to an exhibition at the National Gallery, curated by Colin Painter, in which the approach to Constable's painting *The Cornfield* was mediated by domestic objects. Walker showed works from various projects, addressing the (usually prohibited) sense of touch in the encounter with objects in a museum and introducing the unease of doubt and desire. These included *Mr and Mrs Walker have moved*, at Kettle's Yard, where he, his partner Anne Eggebert, and their small son occupied Jim Ede's house; and *Touch*, at Wolverhampton Art Gallery, where, among other works, Walker touched a painting completely, echoing the video he made at the British Museum, in which hands caress display cases, lingering in an unseemly manner. The 'improper' nature of touch, of desire out of place, is extended in Walker's work with nineteenth-century samplers, as he undoes the stitching to insert his own texts using the recuperated thread. Walker ended with a video of his lecture/performance in which he waltzed with the teeth of King John from the collection of Worcester City Art Gallery, to the tune of 'I danced with a man who danced with a girl who danced with the Prince of Wales', neatly illustrating the lecture series' theme of 'Provenance'.

Contributors	*Jaspar Joseph-Lester, Natassia Page, Nick Stewart*
Chair	*Sharon Kivland*

Audience *Is provenance different from memory? How do objects function? Perhaps, in relation to provenance, objects operate as evidence whereas they perform as triggers in the realms of memory. I am thinking about the status of the photograph…*

JW The photograph is an *aide-mémoire*. Because it's not the real thing, it triggers memory. There is so much that is projected onto objects. The Rosetta Stone, for example, was barely used in deciphering hieroglyphs and yet it represents decoding, the solving of a mystery. People expect that of it and are often disappointed when they find out that Young didn't use it much, that Champollion got there before him. We all have objects that we use as markers – a cultural group of objects – like the big dinosaur in the Natural History Museum, now surrounded by Perspex because so many people pinched bits of it that they couldn't keep up with replicating. Even though it's a cast, it still has a mythic status, reminding people of their childhood, of their first visits to the Natural History Museum. Memory plays an enormous part. How you might separate provenance from memory? We think of provenance as 'this was owned by this person previously'. An object picks up bits of identity like dust or skin cells; presence is transferred to the object. A lot of that you don't know when first you encounter the object, then the object changes. What is happening is a link of memory and the object, but not in linear time. It's jumping into the past. Susan Stewart, in *On Longing*, writes of the physical relic; the relic of the body is so immediate, so challenging to your person that it erases the significance of time.

Audience *This extends the way objects are used in a personal way. There is a difference between a personal object, and what's placed in a wider sphere.*

JW Many objects do function in a personal way. I have a personal stake in the Rosetta Stone because I've grown up with it.

JJ-L *The Chapman brothers' act of painting over Goya's etchings with clown faces seems relevant to some of the things that you discussed. You were talking about the relation between the original and the copy in terms of the reproduction of the original in quite positive terms. You mentioned Walter Benjamin's theory of the aura. How can the reproduction tell us something new, something productive, about the original?*

JW Colin Painter's exhibition at the National Gallery, about Constable's *Cornfield* was interesting in that respect. *The Cornfield* wasn't the first thing you saw. There were tea towels, jigsaw puzzles, wrapping paper; anything you could imagine that was mass-produced with the painting on it. These were shown with photographs of their owners, in their sitting rooms and kitchens. There was a text explaining how each person had acquired these objects and it was clear that many had never seen the painting. I felt that mechanical reproduction could be acting as an obstacle to a real experience of the painting. I made my work *The Acquisitions* of the British Museum at the time the grand court was being designed. When you went into the forecourt of the British Museum, the shop was on your left, then you went up the steps into the main hall to turn left through the cloakroom. Then, turning right into the Egyptian Hall, you faced another shop of souvenirs and postcards, the shops getting smaller and smaller, funneling your person and your mind. There were particular things on sale telling you that these were the important things in the museum. These mediate your experience of the object and, of course, the main one is the Rosetta Stone. I don't know if this is destroying the aura of the original. The souvenir copy doesn't carry the same force as the original but helps you experience an important marker of culture in your life. When these things are in a shop in Heathrow Airport, they're like Franklin Mint plates of Constable's *The Cornfield*. I don't know if they'd serve any purpose at all if they were bought at Tesco, but they would be different than if they were bought at the National Gallery shop. I observed at the National Gallery what people actually do: they look at a painting, then at the label, then at the painting again. The amount of time they spent looking at the painting the second time depends on whether the label has an important name on it. If it is anonymous Dutch painting then they will move to next the one; if it is Rembrandt, they will look for thirty seconds more.

NS   *People fetishize reproductions of painting, especially Constable, because of what the painting signifies through tradition. The painting is a signifier of national identity.*

JW   It does have that attribute. You could include the Rosetta Stone. It is by virtue of conquest through imperial power that we have a lot of the stuff in the British Museum. *The Cornfield* tells people what they want to know about what they would like to see. The sketches for *The Cornfield* show that it is a composite of about fifteen different sources. It would be nice if some of them weren't actually English.

Audience   *It is interesting that you work so closely with institutions and that your interest in objects extends to touching them and living in the museum. Robert Smithson described the museum as a tomb housing dead objects. Are you criticizing gallery or museum attitudes in participating with these objects in a different way?*

JW   It would be biting the hand that feeds me to criticize them. My practice doesn't argue with their conventions but explores why they exist. The curator of the Wellcome Trust Collection wrote about artists in museums, saying that if the privilege of the curator having access is extended to artists, you may just be extending that privilege to another self-elected group. That's a strong criticism. As an artist, I have to justify my privilege through my research. It is a privilege because people don't generally get the opportunity to touch objects, to work with them closely. This is an area where being an artist means not being an artist in the way most people understand the term.

Audience   *In your participation with the objects, especially living in Kettle's Yard, you said you were communicating with the public, so that may open the possibility of wider participation.*

JW   All the works test that. They take away the preserved objecthood of the object, asking what the object really is. Heidegger is good at the historical analysis of the concept of core and attribute, and how the separation between the two aspects of an object can be traced back to Greek and Roman thought.

Audience *You spoke of objects' aspiration to immortality. Does the presence of the viewer grant immortality to an object or is it their physical touch?*

JW It works both ways. The work in Wolverhampton involved touching the painting and also making photographs that replicated the painting with local people. Their images got into a museum collection, with all the implications of preservation for posterity. They get immortality by placing themselves in the space of the object. The replica can gain immortality, like the 'Billys and Charlies' – fake mediaeval artefacts manufactured in the nineteenth century – when they were made, they were considered real. History has brought considerably more of the 'real' originals to light and we return to the idea of value linked to rarity. The potential number of buried originals is larger, and so the 'Billys and Charlies' are more important. When museums can't pay the heating bills, they keep their 'Billys and Charlies' and sell off their originals.

SK *Why are they called 'Billys and Charlies'?*

JW They were made by William Smith and Charles Easton.

NP *As you often exhibit as an artist in a museum, what is the difference between galleries and museums, especially in relation to Mark Dion and his Thames Tate work.*

JW It's worth looking at Mark Dion. How acceptable is it for me to go to a place like Wolverhampton and tell them what their work is about, especially with a work that is municipally owned, considered the pride of their collection, a local painting for local people? My works are made as site-specific works and it's difficult to show them outside the places they were made. The practice is the site. The samplers I alter are the space where I do the work. They concentrate my relation with the person who made them but that only works because it is preserved. I made this work as a project with the Embroiderers' Guild. They were selecting artists who hadn't worked with stitch before. I proposed that I would buy nineteenth-century samplers, take them apart and use the thread to write my own text. They had a long debate and finally decided to accept my project on the condition they retained a veto over which samplers I could use. I had to submit my lists from ebay. I think the first list had fifteen samplers; they vetoed thirteen of them.

Audience *Do you see yourself as an artist working in a museum rather then a curator interfering with museum collections?*

JW Well, I interfere with collections but I don't see myself as a curator. If you apply for a job at the Natural History Museum, you must declare if you have a collection of natural history objects and if you do, you have to get rid of them. You have to preserve your purity of soul. It's a conflict of interests.

SK *The idea that the museum preserves is not entirely true. The V&A had a large collection of embroideries from the eighteenth century in stump-work, where the cloth is gathered up. These clumps are carefully undone, because in them, the cloth is as it was when it was printed, and so is of great interest to historians.*

JW Can you imagine the embarrassment of the people who collected the 'Billys and Charlies' for the British Museum, when they were revealed to be fakes? They were dismissed to the furthest corner of the deepest cellar. Yet they change; they come back again. It's not static. Museums do get rid of things. The word 'museum' comes from the phrase 'the temple of the muses' in classical Greece. People donated objects to the temple of the muses, which were buried, kept for posterity. In a time of crisis you were allowed to dig them up and melt them down to pay your army but you had to repay it with interest. When you won the battle, you would have to give back more to the temple of the muses.

Audience *I love this mercurial shifting of objects to site. I like to think that the reason some people didn't eat the chocolate you distributed, was not that it was unhygienic but because it was a relic of an art event. What interests me is how you negotiate between the work as the document and as the original site.*

JW Once you say 'now', it's gone. Now doesn't exist so where is the work? Can it exist as anything other than memory or experience? The documentation can only serve as an *aide-mémoire* or as the art object itself. I suspect that it becomes two things. *Dancing with King John's Teeth* is a video, there's my experience of the work as an art object and the experience of the people who were sitting in the audience, eating or not eating the chocolate. I like making something that changes people.

Audience *I don't object to the thing or the object or the event of the object. What concerns me is how these object-events would take place without your narrative.*

JW You have had an unreal experience because you've seen only part of my work with a spiel that most people in the gallery would not have. But they would know the history of those objects. When they come away, they lose a bit and they need help and that comes from several sources, a gloss, written conscious of the fact that people only read a hundred and eighty words on a label, or the Internet. It's a bit like expecting to go to a restaurant and not reading the menu. Why shouldn't we expect people to read before they experience the works?

The work is not only about looking. When I'm preparing a work, I take photographs, I write and I negotiate verbally with the site; that's part of the preparation process. Making the work involves words, so it's reasonable to expect people to engage with the work textually.

Audience *Does it matter that we couldn't clearly hear the dialogue between you and the woman whom you were trying to palm the plate off at Kettle's Yard? I was thinking of you buying samplers on ebay. All that may be just as interesting as the work itself. How do you make decisions about what to include?*

JW It is quite difficult to decide how much of a voice to give the institution. You could see from my gestures what is going on, but I also assumed that work would be seen by people who would know about collections and institutions. In *Touch*, the touching of the picture would suggest that inherent in the work is the negotiation of permission. The presence of the institution is implicit. It's like those exhibitions when they analyze the different layers of paint on a seventeenth-century painting and they work out Rembrandt's income from the materials that were used in the paints. The work carries its history in the same way an object carries its history.

SK *When you were trying to donate the plate to Kettles Yard, did the woman answering the door to you know that you're an artist and not a mad person?*

JW I told her that I was going to bring something to the door and try and get her to accept it, (this happens). I asked her to go through her normal practice in that situation. I tried to persuade her and she said that it was a closed collection. It worked in the first take. In a sense, it's not a work of art because if she had said they'd take it, I would've said, 'oh great, thank you'.

Audience *Role-play occupies the same site as the replica because when people become engaged in role-play they believe that that is the authentic event or experience.*

JW I felt the third photograph of the Wolverhampton series was more beautiful than the original painting because the people really cared about taking part in its re-staging. In the painting the eldest son has his hand on his sword, and in the re-staging, a man in his sixties stood in the same position. He put his hand in his pocket. It looked perfect. I felt that the role-playing was on a par with the reality of the picture.

EC *I'm intrigued by the relationship you have with the teams in the museum, making them witnesses to your activities. How integral are the rules and the regulations, the curators as audience to your practice? It seems as if you put them in quite an uncomfortable position, not only in terms of risk of damage to the objects but also to their provenance.*

JW They do have a problem of whether they should be seen or not seen. Incidentally, I'm aware that my privilege rests on that I'm white, male, middle-class and well-educated. I come from the same background as these people; I speak their language. If you don't, I'm sure they would be more suspicious. Negotiations are very delicate.

EC *I wasn't so much thinking of the practicalities, but of the sensitivities in the languages you use, particularly with the touching piece where you talk about intrusion or violation. There is a sexual undercurrent. The idea of sleeping with a collection is provocative.*

JW I didn't see the sexual content till I was putting image and word together: I am sleeping with the museum. Similarly, I find the samplers problematic, intruding on a girl child's work. For a long time that stopped me making these works. At the British Museum, the curator with whom I was working filmed that work, so in a sense it's the museum's gaze on me in the museum – not to say I could blame him if anything goes wrong but he is rendered complicit. There have been many situations where I have been told I can't do something. I wanted to move into Huddersfield Art Gallery, taking objects from the collections and using them as they were intended, making a home there. I wanted to sleep on a nineteenth-century campaign bed. The art curator agreed but the museum curators didn't, so it didn't happen.

Audience *The work you did in Hastings with the feathered mask felt ritualistic, like objects you might use in shamanistic practice. How has ritual influenced you?*

JW There is a problem with ritual objects because once they are removed to the museum, they stop being ritual objects. In the Museum of Mankind, I used a necklace from a culture that didn't practise material inheritance. When a person died, their possessions were buried with them. The museum showed an ethnographic object that denied the ethnography that it was attempting to illustrate. So it has two histories: its history as an anthropological object and as a museum object. Objects in a collection obtain a formal identity that overrides their individual identity. This is the problem with shamanistic objects; they are de-fused.

Audience *Do you mind if there isn't a physical object that persists after the event? Do you want that object as a work or is it more that you need the evidence?*

JW The documentation at Kettle's Yard is a poor second to the experience of the work, which was about living in the space. I have spoken a lot about *King John's Teeth*, but that's the first time I've shown the video. I showed it to my partner but she fell asleep. Ten people were in the audience and they are the only other people who have seen it. I intend to make it as a work, but it will be a different thing because I won't have King John's teeth.

Nick Stewart
Flayed House 1
2005
DV still

24.11.04 **Nick Stewart**

Whether in early work with performance and installation, more recent video works, or in current digital image and publishing projects, Nick Stewart has always responded to the actuality of place and the people living there. This lecture focused on the strand of his work related to his Irish identity. While he presented earlier work in a chronological sequence of slides and video in a split-screen presentation, the other part of the screen showed changing fragments of text, drawn from his current work-in-progress, *No-One's Not From Everywhere*. This is a book and exhibition project of sampled texts from recorded conversations with a large number of Irish artists, both living in Ireland and abroad.

Stewart emphasized that the theme of Irish identity, running through his work over the past twenty years, was not conceived of as a single body of work. Rather, he sought to draw a line through his work in drawing, performance, video and installation, to connect and assess it, relating the concerns of modernism to the conflicts of identity as experienced in Northern Ireland. Stewart, quoting Thomas McEvilley from *Art and Discontent*, suggested that the resonance of any work of art lies in the context of 'both the viewer's and the artist's sensibilities, with all the conditioning and acculturation involved in them: 'It exists in other words, not as an isolated absolute or an end in itself but as a rounded cultural object which relates to philosophy, politics, psychology, religion and so forth.' He spoke of his rejection of formalist sculpture in the early 1980s and his move to process-based work of a more temporary nature. Stewart showed a number of works that demonstrated that while where he is from has both coloured his life and his art, his work strenuously avoids autobiography. But he acknowledged that many earlier pieces sublimated questions of identity in images of confinement, of restriction and of 'boundedness' that reflected something of the socio-political reality of living in Northern Ireland at the time.

Contributors   *John Clark, Emma Cocker, Nayan Kulkarni, Alice Maude-Roxby, Hazel Turner-Lyons*
Chair   *Sharon Kivland*

AM-R   *I am interested both in the status of the documentation of your performance work and your own role as the subject of that documentation.*

NS   I never felt like I was the subject of the documentation of those performances. Yes, it was I engaged in whatever action, but 'I' was not the subject of the work. In fact that's one of the main reasons I stopped doing them. In the late 80s there was more and more emphasis on the performer as an actor rather than as someone simply carrying out a task. I wasn't at all interested in that new theatricality in performance. Yes, I was interested in the performativity of the everyday: those 'found' situations in the city where there is a fortuitous conjunction of place and people. This is something that still engages me. It represents a shift from understanding performance as something carried out by a performer, to performance as a quality of everyday life. The writings of Richard Schechner on performance were influential in developing this understanding.

The more recent shift towards a text-based practice relates to an increasing problem I'm having with the image. I just don't want to work with images at the moment. I'm interested in text as something that involves the reader at other levels than just the visual. The reader must think their way into and through the text. Also, the sort of texts I'm interested in leave a lot of space for the reader to construct their own reading, to find their own meaning, in the work. The idea of sampling informs much of my interest in this at the moment. I'm interested in the complex relation of a number of fragments of text, open ended and extended, suggesting a continuous process of reading and thinking rather than simply beginning and ending, as in a more conventional narrative.

JC *The unrealised proposal for the derelict cottage in the courtyard of the Museum of Modern Art in Dublin reminded me that often the research that informs a work can be more interesting than the resulting work. Do you think it is important that the work is actually made?*

NS I don't know if it is important if any work gets made. I can only do what I feel is the right thing to do. But if a work is conceived to involve people in an actual place, in relation to actual objects and images, in a particular form, then it is hardly comparable to simply substitute the idea itself. I'm not a conceptual artist. Certainly, in relation to this particular building, I would very much have liked to carry out this piece. The experience of people visiting it would be hugely different to simply presenting it as a drawing and text, say. It is an actual building with a particularly resonant history and as such is to be experienced as much as simply thought about.

NK *I am interested in ideas of distance that seemed to come out of the lecture. There seemed to be two distinct formations: one of time and geographical location and the other as a more formal discursive protocol that you appear to have set up for the publication project. I am specifically interested in the conception and detail of the protocol and its description to the artists when you contacted them. Also, I am interested in hearing a little more about how time and dislocation may (or may not) have opened up the space for the project. It also seems to be a very opportune time for an artist to be exploring these themes in the forms that you are taking. Any comments?*

NS If you come from a place where even the distance of one short street can mean a transition from one community to another and where to 'put a foot wrong', so to speak, can mean real danger, then of course, you become very aware of your place in relation to those communities. So, when I left Northern Ireland the sense of freedom I experienced was profound. Not everyone from the north might have that, I know. But for me it was a real release from what had become an increasingly claustrophobic living situation. With time, the distance opened up between that previous life there and my new life in London, has given me a different perspective on my identity. I am now able to confront some things, address questions, consider images, I would not before have allowed myself to.

For the *No-One's Not From Everywhere* project I have been very particular in the kind of situations I've been setting up with Irish artists. I wanted to meet and talk with as broad a cross-section of Irish artists as I could, to discuss our conception and experience of home, place, community and so on, in relation to the conventional images of Irish identity. It is not my intention to author a thesis on the subject. It will be, when all is said and done, an artist's book project.

The recordings I've made were not of interviews. They were of conversations, usually three-way and in an informal, social setting, often with food and drink, in someone's flat or a pub. The artists were told that any material sampled from the resulting recordings would not be credited. It would be anonymous. I wanted people to feel free to say anything without fear of quotation. I also promised all participants that the mini-discs would be destroyed after the project was finished. The text resulting from all this is being distilled from the participation of some fifty Irish artists and will be designed to involve a parallel visual dimension for the work. The intention is to create a complex text of sampled fragments. A paragraph in *Very Little... Almost Nothing: Death, Philosophy, Literature* by Simon Critchley is very relevant in relation to this:

> We might say provisionally that what the form of the fragment opens up is the possibility of discontinuous writing. An ensemble of fragments – for a fragment is never written in isolation – is a discontinuous and uneven field. Texts of varying length and worth are typographically, if not thematically, organized across intervals and this lends a certain staccato rhythm or abrupt musicality to their reading... An ensemble of fragments can treat a potentially infinite number of topics that do not have to stand in any agreement or constitute any coherent argument but simply testify to the unceasing alternation and differentiation of thoughts. Fragments are traces of an intense and agile aphoristic energy, a power of absolutely unlimited extension and intensity... The fragment opens up the possibility of collective and anonymous writing... The

future is faced with fragments, with fragments of an impossible future, a future that itself appears fragmentary.

As you say, the timing seems opportune. This is yet another moment in Irish history when the debate about who we are is reaching some kind of critical point.

HT-L *Something that struck me when looking at your work was the remarkable feeling of identification I had with it. Being born out of wedlock to a man from Northern Ireland and a woman from Stoke, growing up in East London and now living in Sheffield, I too have often pondered this question of 'home'. A curious symptom of this is that I often find myself feeling nostalgic for events and places that have nothing to do with me, such as the closure of the steelworks in Sheffield. Also, the moment I tell people that my dad was born in Belfast they say, dismissively, 'oh, but not the real Ireland'. Real Ireland?*

NS It's been amazing for me to discover through these conversations with Irish artists how many different perceptions of authenticity there are in relation to Irishness and different places in Ireland. There simply is no consensus as to what 'real' Ireland is or, for that matter, what a 'real' Irish person might be. Thankfully. That is part of my intention: to make complex that which is so often reduced to stereotype and cliché.

HT-L *You talked about becoming tired of performance art, which was a relatively new medium for art, particularly those involving charged political issues, in the 1980s. First of all, do you think that performance art has become dated – for want of a better word – and, if it has indeed become dated, do you believe it has it been consigned to the past along with the issues that it sought to deal with? Also, do you think that the medium of performance will always carry with it those associations?*

NS Tired is not quite the right word. It was more the feeling that something that was fresh had become somewhat mannered. It felt like a certain trajectory of performance art had become predictable. This wasn't so much a personal feeling. It was something that was in the air at that time. A number of artists known for their performance work shifted more towards images and objects and away from live performance. There was some dissatisfaction with the encroachment of visual theatre into the context of performance art. I certainly felt uneasy with the sense that the emphasis was shifting from the art bit to the performance bit. I didn't see myself as a performer, rather someone who carried out certain tasks at certain times. The development of video, which had become much cheaper and easier to use also contributed to this shift. I was on a residency at the Western Front in Vancouver in early 1990 and they insisted that all their residents made a video during their stay. That was a turning point for me. I found that using the camera was a performative activity. I also became interested in the performative quality of people's behaviour in the city. The framing of specific architectural spaces and people in those spaces became a central concern of the work at that point. Since then it seems that performance has been sublimated into mainstream practice. Many of the better-known artists of the past ten or more years have incorporated the performative into their work; Gillian Wearing, Mark Wallinger, the Wilson twins. You know them all. Isn't this what happens in art? It's no great insight to say that yesterday's radical practice is today's mainstream. But it is generally true. In the past couple of years it seems that performance as a distinct medium is reasserting itself. So what goes around comes around.

NK *There seemed to be some tension in the texts between Nick Stewart as the author, editing texts as a kind of film and the authors as speakers. At what point does the voice cease to be a voice and become a text? It seemed to me that it was much more complex than the simple transformation from the space of speech to the space of transcription.*

NS That's something I had to consider very carefully. I was aware of that tension from the moment I conceived of the project. It was something I discussed with each participant because I knew that they would also be considering it. I suppose I could be quite literal about this and say that the voice becomes a text at precisely the point where I make the editorial decision to extract it from the stream of recorded conversation and crystallize it as a text. At that point its context shifts from that of the conversation to that of the page and a relation to many other fragments of text. It floats free of its source and develops new associations with other texts. This is where my interest lies in this project. The conversations were important for me on a personal level. They were by turns, confrontational, intimate, revealing and much more. There was a point where I thought they were actually the work. But now, having listened to the many hours of recordings, I can view them more objectively. The task has been to sample fragments from these but without necessarily understanding the relation of one fragment to another. The next stage was to begin to assemble these fragments in a new relation, one that precisely looks at this question of identity from as many different angles as possible. The sense of different voices speaking is still important but the trajectory of a conversation has been abandoned. It will be the task of the reader to take a position in relation to the content. I will not be drawing any conclusions for them. I am not attempting to prove a thesis.

EC   *I am interested in the relation between editing and censorship, and the connections between sampling and intentionality where you gather interviews as a book work. How aware are you of privileging certain voices and silencing others as you edit and order?*

NS   Just to clarify, these were not interviews. I don't want to seem pedantic about this but the form of these meetings was an important part of the project that I considered at length. I discussed the project with all the participants. Everyone understood the nature of what they were entering into. I can make an analogy with video. When someone is videoed they usually understand that editing will take place. No one is quoted by name so in that sense all quotes are the textual fragments are equal. The reader will read them as uncredited quotes. This was again an important part of the methodology and everyone participated in full knowledge of it. Of course I am privileging certain quotes. From each recording, which ran from one to four hours in duration with different participants, I only sampled, at most, three pages. Usually just one or two. So the bulk of what was said was discarded. Nevertheless I don't see this process as privileging or silencing. It might just as easily be said to be enhancing. When all is said and done, I don't have a problem with authoring the work, or indeed, with privileging certain content, though it is important to consider that this text will not record just a single point of view. Quite the opposite. It's hard to be an artist and not make such decisions. If we didn't take such risks our work would just be bland and uneventful.

EC   *You also choose to offer your own position. You talked about a coded dialogue, using colour to trace routes and make connections. Is there a dilemma in attempting to offer a particular viewpoint, whilst trying to achieve or allow for the interplay, for contradiction?*

NS   I'm colour coding text but not to offer a 'particular viewpoint'. Connections will be made for any number of reasons but these connections will not make a thesis, so to speak. In fact contradiction will be at the heart of the choices I make. Colour coding and the other editing decisions I make are at the service of the idea of placing the reader as the focus of the work. The reader does the work of reading. Precisely. I only want to provide as complex a reading experience as possible for that reader.

SK   *Where do you feel at home now?*

NS   London is my home now. It's a city full of people from everywhere in the world, most of whom are not 'at home' here. It's the opposite of everything I was brought up with. I could not live anywhere else, without such diversity. Ireland is the home I cannot be at home in.

Nick Stewart
Flayed House 2
2005
DV still

Location, Location, Location:
Provenance and the Place of Art

Steve Edwards

Provenance is a term with a complex lineage in the history of art
and archaeology: its meaning is tied up with place of origin. The Latin
root *provenire* literally means to come forth. Presumably, this setting
out requires a location from which to embark. I want to offer some,
more-or-less, haphazard thoughts on provenance and the place of art.
My aim is simply to advance a few reflections on three orders of
provenance, which turn out to involve three oddly dislocated places.
A critic might deem, with some justification, that I am playing out a
little structural game.

Location

Provenance is most familiar to art history from the work of the
connoisseur and the operation of the auction house. As a model
of art historical scholarship, connoisseurship was at its height at the
end of the nineteenth century and the early years of the twentieth
century, but it remains a core procedure for dealers and auctioneers:
the connoisseur and the sales room are linked by more than just the
metaphor of value. As Carlo Ginzburg understood, the connoisseur's
vision is practical rather than interpretive: it revolves around
attributing an art work to a period, school or particular artist; it entails
distinguishing between the hand of a master and that of an apprentice;
or spotting the difference between an original and a fake.[1]

One key way for the connoisseur to situate the art work centres
on stylistic analysis: think of Morelli's typology of ears and fingernails
in Renaissance painting as indices of particular masters; or consider
Berenson pouring over his black and white photographs in order to
attribute works to an oeuvre. For Max J. Friedländer the key task of
the connoisseur was to link particular works to a 'personality'. He
went so far as to claim that 'nameless pieces mostly are valueless and

devoid of character'.[2] But, if the central task of connoisseurship is to authenticate the work by attributing it to a particular artist, the places through which an object has circulated provide significant clues for that task. Embodied in exhibition and sales catalogues as well as the related scholarly *catalogue raisonné*, the task of the connoisseur is, as one short definition of provenance has it, to 'keep track of an art work'.[3] Knowing where the art work has been is central to the connoisseur's job of ratifying, authenticating and ultimately certifying artistic commodities. In this sense, connoisseurial inquiry is structured around an idea of the place of origin, since it involves locating the art work: ultimately to a particular studio, at a circumscribed period and hence to the hand of a master.

There seems to be a second sense of place at work in this connoisseurial notion of provenance, because particular places appear as sites for the circulation of value: a series of great houses through which the work of art passes.[4] (Museums with their typical neo-classical buildings and flock wallpaper, which replicate the homes of aristocratic patrons, serve as modern displacements for those other private sites.) The art work and the building confer value on one another: and these sites with their itineraries and documents provide secure marks of ownership in the quest for provenance. Ultimately, the connoisseur would prefer to establish an unbroken chain of ownership in which the art work passes from hand to hand and place to place, all the way back to the original act of acquisition in the studio (ideally, at this point of purchase, the paint would still be wet or the statue covered in a fine layer of marble dust). The connoisseur aims, in this way, to fashion a metonymic chain that stretches unbroken to an artistic personality.

In connoisseurship, then, provenance seems to securely denote two kinds of place: a place of origin and the places of circulation. In another sense, however, provenance undergoes a peculiar dislocation, because both orders of place lead back to a desire called 'Florence' or 'Venice'. The key reference here is to another inveterate connoisseur – of people as well as works of art – Marcel Proust. One could travel to these places to visit, and the experts did, but Proust recognised that the proper names of Renaissance cities acted as magnets for 'desire', or 'longing'.[5] Actual place was subordinated to an aesthetic transformation shaped by guidebooks, art magazines and travellers' tales. These 'countries which we long for occupy, at any given moment, a far larger place in our actual life than the country in which we happen to be'. For him, this desire was predicated on its real proximity or availability, while simultaneously short-circuiting fulfilment. The transformative dimension to connoisseurship turns on this displacement, where the strange place that is the imaginary Renaissance created an aesthetic space in the present: a space for 'the life not yet lived, the life intact and pure'. Proust, particularly as his health declined, studied art and architecture largely through photographs. He wrote to a friend that he was now unable to visit his cherished cathedrals, but 'by means of your precious photographs', they 'pay me the visit I used to make so often to them?'[6] The metonymic form of the photograph was central to this aesthetic dislocation since, through it, one could travel without leaving home.[7] For this reason Friedländer feared the photograph. In contrast Walter Benjamin – a translator and avid reader of Proust – could see that this displacement of provenance through photographic proximity could be given radical turn.[8]

Location

The forms of place embedded in connoisseurship underwent a fundamental transformation with the emergence of modernism. In the connoisseur's purview art was entwined with the desire called 'Italy': the desire called 'Paris' was of a different order. Some of the low and illicit pleasures might be the same (or similar enough), but Paris had come to name a peculiarly dislocated place all its own. In the modernist imagination Paris occupied a place akin to its situation in the Surrealist map of the world – *The World in the Time of the Surrealists* of 1929 – where France disappeared leaving behind only its capital relocated in Germany. This anti-chauvinist gesture was, in the wider culture of modernism, generalised so that Paris became a chronotope: 'Paris, Capital of the Nineteenth Century'; Paris, the 'International of Culture'.

Perhaps the best guide to this chronotopic capital is Harold Rosenberg's essay 'The Fall of Paris', written in 1940.[9] Rosenberg was reflecting, in hindsight, on the role of Paris in modernist culture: he wrote at the point when the Nazi occupation had shut down what he called 'the laboratory of the twentieth century'. But prior to this fall, Paris, he claimed, had been 'possessed by the searchers of every nation':

> By Picasso and Juan Gris, Spaniards; by Modigliani, Boccioni and Severini, Italians; by Brancusi, Rumanian; by Joyce, Irishman; by Mondrian, Dutchman; by Lipchitz, Polish Lithuanian; by Archipenko,

Kandinsky, Diaghilev, Larionov, Russians; by Calder, Pound, Gertrude
Stein, Man Ray, Americans; by Kupka, Czechoslovak; Lehmbruck
and Max Ernst, Germans; by Wyndham Lewis and T. E. Hulme,
Englishmen... by all artists, students refugees.

He seems to have missed the Hungarians, Japanese, Mexicans...; he
doesn't mention that some of these persons were Jewish, and he omits
those others who were black. But we get the idea. All these people
gathered in Paris to fashion an international culture. For Rosenberg,
this culture had 'a definite style: the Modern'.

The 'School of Paris', he argued, belonged to no country; rather it
was 'world-wide and world-timed'. The International modernist style
was intended to transcend place and, to this extent, it appeared devoid
of provenance. Artists could draw on African artefacts and Japanese
prints, folk art or Iberian sculpture, these forms mattered in so far as
they distanced the modernist international from the actual place in
which it was sited. That is to say, particular or local traditions served
to mark Paris off from itself. Although it developed in New York, the
white space of the modernist museum seems like a perfect homology
for this displaced culture; as does that other modernist obsession
with that ultimate in placelessness – the airplane.[10] In his strongest
formulation Rosenberg claimed that 'the Paris Modern... produced a
No-Time, and the Paris "International" a No-Place'. That is to say, the
place without provenance figured Utopia.[11]

Paris, then, was the place that was not one. For a while New York
would occupy the same paradoxical spot. Nevertheless, the problem
of provenance would return in strange ways to mark this modernist
international. Even more than in the connoisseurial model the lure
of 'personality' played a central role in modernism. Whereas place
had previously served to certify the art work, here biography provided
the ultimate locus for legitimation. Even if the same tale was told
over and over, an artist's life story supplied the ground for meaning
and value. Modernist biography is a peculiarly self-contained form,
which posits a self as origin while refusing its particularity. The self
that inhabits the modernist international is largely interchangeable.
Another form of modernist provenance is found in high modernist
theory, where the tradition itself took on the form of lineage and
defined historical legitimacy.

Location
Space and place are everywhere in contemporary art and culture. As

Neil Smith and Cindi Katz put it:

> The breadth of interest in space is matched by the breadth of spatial
> metaphors in vogue... spatial metaphors have become a predominant
> means by which social life is understood. 'Theoretical spaces' have been
> 'explored', 'mapped', 'charted', 'contested', 'de-colonized' and everyone
> seems to be 'travelling'. [12]

We could add to this list: 'site', 'location', 'dislocation', 'geographies',
'borders', 'zones', 'migration', 'exile', and so on. This spatial vision seems
to be encapsulated by the title of Homi Bhabha's book: *The Location
of Culture*.[13] Culture now seems to be defined by its place; to find it
we are required to look beyond the standard spaces of the European
tradition. It is unlikely that it will turn out to be integral.

It is now a commonplace to suggest that this recent concern
with place – in particular, place beyond the Western 'centre' – has
developed alongside the increasingly integrated capitalist economy
and the communications networks that are closely linked to it.
International Biennale culture – Venice, Istanbul, Johannesburg,
Havana, 'Documenta', 'Manifesta' and the rest – provides a cultural lens
for these tendencies. Over the last ten years these mega-exhibitions
have, at a single venue (or, at least, a number of venues across a
single city) drawn together works from diverse geographical zones.
Sometimes, works seem to be included simply because they attest to
the experience of particular places. It is certainly the case that the key
conception of these exhibitions is cumulative or additive: their collage
structure builds a homology for this new world order, which insists on
both the proximity and the distance separating places and cultures. In
this sense, the biennales seem to internalise the structure of the world
economy, with its proximities of time and space, its flows and relays,
its drive to integrate and fragment. But the version of this state of
affairs that emerges on the ground of the biennales appears as if it has
undergone processing by some strange Duchampian engine.

Once again provenance seems to occupy the centre ground in
recent cultural practice where the artist has become a bearer of place.
Perhaps, the strangest phenomenological experience had in these
exhibitions is the perpetual switch of languages as a projection in
Chinese gives way to a Japanese animation work or an Albanian video.
In this sense, biennale culture appears to be constantly throwing up
new towers of Babel. It is not clear, however, whether these
exhibitions provide that way of 'inhabiting one's culture', called for

by Paul Willemen, which would be 'neither myopically nationalist nor evasively cosmopolitan'.[14] The problem here seems to be the simultaneous concern with attesting to place and the understandable refusal of national tradition or pure experience. In this sense, contemporary culture seems to be built on an antimony – a staging of place that is accompanied by a simultaneous drive to empty it out. The current concern with sampling, mixing, blending, fluidity, impurity, and hybridity all attest to this dual impulse: these categories require national traditions or local idioms to put through the cultural blender. As such, cultural form must appear both integral and fractured, placed and displaced. Okwui Enwezor describes this form as 'transnational'.[15] He may well be right, but it is also possible that we are again in the presence of a Utopian International; albeit one that has cast its net significantly wider than happened with 'Paris'. If it has a 'definite style', this time it is one linked to the space and time of the video projector.

1   Carlo Ginzburg, 'Clues: Roots of an Evidential Paradigm', *Myths, Emblems, Clues*, London: Hutchinson Radius 1990, pp.96-125.

2   Max J. Friedländer, *On Art and Connoisseurship*, London: Bruno Cassirer 1942, p.162.

3   'Provenance', Shearer West ed., *The Bulfinch Guide to Art History*, Boston: Bulfinch 1996, p.731.

4   A third version of place would turn on the idea of 'national schools' and 'national character'. For an examination of nationalism in art history see: Christopher S. Wood, 'Introduction', *The Vienna School Reader: Politics and Art Historical Method in the 1930s*, Cambridge, Mass: Zone Books 2000, pp.9-72.

5   Marcel Proust, *Remembrance of Things Past*, Vol. 1, Harmondsworth: Penguin 1983, pp.419-27.

6   Cited in Brassaï, *Proust in the Power of Photography*, Chicago: The University of Chicago Press 2001, pp.29-30.

7   My key reference for this radical structure of the aesthetic journey is Jacques Rancière, *Short Voyages to the Land of the People*, Stanford: Stanford University Press 2003.

8   Walter Benjamin, 'The Work of Art in the Age of its Technological Reproducibility: Second Version', *Walter Benjamin: Selected Writings*, Volume 3, 1935-38, Cambridge: The Belknap Press 2002, pp.101-33.

9   Harold Rosenberg, 'The Fall of Paris', *The Tradition of the New*, London: Paladin 1970, pp.185-94.

10 Anthony Vidler, *Warped Space: Art, Architecture, and Anxiety in Modern Culture*, Cambridge, Mass: MIT 2000, pp.178-9.

11 Internationalism is pretty unfashionable these days so it should be said that this urge to overcome the local and the particular – be it in the international style in architecture, abstract painting, Esperanto or the Communist International – was founded on a genuinely radical desire. The impetus of internationalism was not convergence – it was not a fantasy of merger, though it was sometimes that – but the desire to overcome nationalism and petty provincialism. It does not seem clear to me, in a time of revivified nationalism and a resurgent religious right, that the current preoccupation with difference and identity is self-evidently more radical or critical than this drive to create a place beyond place. Failure may have been likely: given the conjuncture, inevitable even, but the effort was no worse for all that.

12 Neil Smith and Cindi Katz, 'Grounding Metaphor – Towards a Spatialized Politics', Michael Keith and Steve Pile, *Place and the Politics of Identity*, London: Routledge 1993, p.68.

13 Homi Bhabha, *The Location of Culture*, London: Routledge 1994.

14 Paul Willemen, 'The Third Cinema Question', *Looks and Frictions: Essays in Cultural Studies and Film Theory*, Bloomington: British Film Institute/Indiana University Press,1994, p.177.

15 Okwui Enwezor, 'Mega-Exhibitions and the Antinomies of a Transnational Global Form', *MJ – Manifesta Journal*, no.2, Amsterdam, Winter 2003/Spring 2004, pp.6-31.

Inscription

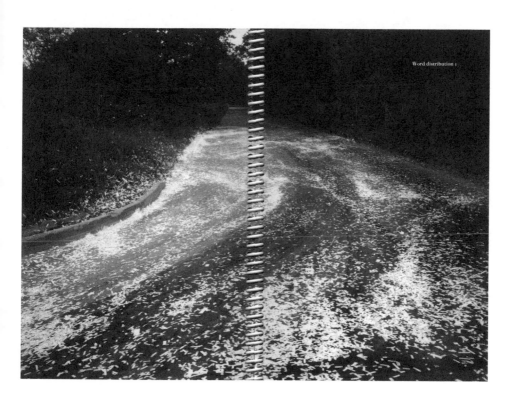

Word distribution 1

Preceding page:
Simon Morris
Pages from *The Royal Road to the Unconscious*
2004
Book
Dimensions when open: 32 x 24 cm

Simon Morris

Simon Morris is a lecturer and artist, whose work includes the *bibliomania* project, *interpretation* and *The Royal Road to the Unconscious*. He has exhibited across Europe and North America and his work can be viewed at *www.informationasmaterial.com*.

Morris began his lecture with a quote from Sol Lewitt, 'Irrational thoughts should be followed absolutely and logically'. He then took the audience through his project *The Royal Road to the Unconscious*, while showing continuously on one side of the projection screen his students painstakingly cutting up Sigmund Freud's *The Interpretation of Dreams*, reading out each word as it was cut from its page. Morris took American artist Ed Ruscha's book *Royal Road Test* (1966) as a set of ready-made instructions, after his attention was arrested by a certain phrase while reading Freud's work, 'The interpretation of dreams is the royal road to a knowledge of the unconscious activities of the mind.' The combination of 'royal' and 'road' reminded him of Ruscha's work, and the seemingly trivial association between the words, used both by Freud and Ruscha, gave him the means by which to subject Freud's text to a random act of madness, what Morris called 'the aleatory moment', set against 'the rigid symbolic corset' of procedural devices that eliminated decisions. Morris proposed that his project followed a logic of the unconscious, with the precedents both of Duchamp's ready-mades and the history of cut-ups, from Tristran Tzara to Brion Gysin and William Burroughs. He suggested that the poetic act of liberating Freud's text entered the domain of the Real, following the work of the psychoanalyst Jacques Lacan, a domain that can neither be imagined nor symbolized. Morris emphasized the importance of collaboration in his practice, and the blurring of distinctions between artist and curator, describing his role as one of establishing theoretical parameters for others, creating a space of transference in which both parties must be open to the encounter. He raised questions of authorship, suggesting that his practice is entirely constructed by his reading or misreading – of other people's art works.

Contributors Silvia Brandstetter, John Clark, Emma Cocker, Emily Cooper, Tom Newell
Chair Sharon Kivland

JC *Have you prepared an answer to this question?*
SM I've got a couple of answers here, yes. What's the question?
JC *That's it. Have you prepared an answer to this question?*
SM John Cage had five prepared answers for his 'Lecture on Nothing' that he read out, whatever was asked.[1] This is my prepared answer: Christian Boltanski says, 'I try to make pieces that are open to interpretation, to tell a story. I have no answers and I'm completely lost. I'm lost in my life, I'm lost in my work, I'm lost everywhere. The only thing we can do is to question, but there are no answers. It is better not to have the answer, because the answers are always so dangerous. There are always so many answers. If someone thinks they

know the answer, they are very dangerous. It is very difficult to speak about your own work, because perhaps it is better not to speak about art, but to look at it, because it is very difficult to explain everything. I'm sure there are plenty of things in my work I don't know. There are plenty of things in my own work I can't explain, and everyone must find their own way to look at it.' I have only two prepared answers, so I hope I don't have three questions.

ECk   *I find read papers quite difficult to engage with. You presented your material without gaps, both visually and textually. But the ideas propose gaps. There is an interesting tension between the proposition of gaps and that you leave none.*

SM   The psychoanalyst talks about lack, the void we have to cover. There is my own nervousness in preparing this for today. However carefully I craft my writing, I know damn well that when I read it – and I did a lot of reading today – it's rubbish. As a lecturer, I know one of the worst things you can do is read a text to the audience. It's very hard for people to listen or engage with material presented in this way. Often the best lectures are when you depart from the material. Luckily my folder fell off the table so I had to stop reading.

ECk   *It wasn't a criticism. There was really an exciting tension between the ideas and the presentation.*

SM   For my PhD thesis, which I'm submitting at the moment, I have had to write twenty thousand words to contextualise my practice. I am fascinated by the pass in Lacanian psychoanalysis. It's like some crazy art work; you never actually meet the panel to which you are presenting your work. You have to present your analysis to two people at the same level of analysis as yourself. They then take that material and then present it to a panel in your absence. This is fantastic. I've written twenty thousand words and I've asked Sharon if I can talk with her about this thesis. I will carefully transcribe our conversation. Then I'm going to turn my text white so that my voice completely disappears. It leaves a gap, hopefully more than I've done today. It leaves a gap for the reader within the conversation. I like the idea that I will never have actually presented my words to the university panel. It will have been written 'through' me, following the methodology I'm talking about, rather than 'by' me.

SK   *I don't know what demon possessed me, but I agreed. It's going to take three and a half-hours, you told me.*

SM   Yes, three and a half-hours. I've been influenced by Kenneth Goldsmith, who is a fantastic American artist.[2] Not only is he director of an amazing site, *www.ubu.com*, the largest Visual, Concrete and Sound Poetry online resource in the world, but he also makes some extraordinary books. In *Soliloquy*, he recorded every word he spoke for an entire week; a hundred and eighty three thousand six hundred and eighty-five words. He speaks three times as fast as I do – so you can imagine – he is a big talker. It took him eight weeks to transcribe one week of his conversation. He wanted to see how much his speech weighed and it weighed five pounds and was four hundred and eighty seven pages long. He spent eight hours a day for eight weeks transcribing it. Goldsmith then asked me to write a preface for a trade edition of this publication. I decided to use Derrida's model of – I think it's called 'Ulysses' Gramophone' – he says you don't stand outside the work you're criticizing, rather you get inside the text, using the methodology of the text to criticize the text from within. What I liked about Kenneth's work was the missing voice. I arranged with Pavel Büchler that we should telephone each other at three o'clock one afternoon to talk for an hour about Kenneth's *Soliloquy*. I rang him, filming myself at my end. Pavel had his team of camera people working with him at his end. Then he sent the tape to me, I transcribed it and the idea was that this would go as bookends to Goldsmith's text. Of course it was rejected, our fifty-nine minute conversation ended up being sixteen pages of text – far too long – it doesn't actually exist as a work as such. However, it was interesting to have these two halves of a conversation. The listener can only hear one half. I remember saying to Pavel, 'Can you imagine yourself as Kenny's wife?' and he said, 'I don't know what you mean, Simon. I can't imagine myself as Kenny's wife.' I said, 'Well, his dog then...' It's like when we see a film and imagine ourselves as Leonardo DiCaprio snogging Kate Winslett or as Kate Winslett snogging Leonardo DiCaprio. You can flick between several subject positions as a spectator. I find that very interesting.

ECp *I'm interested in the idea of the gap and the way you might project what you desire into it. When you spoke about your difficulty in displaying the work in different locations, I wondered if that is the problem with conceptual art, because the work isn't actually what is in the gallery. I think you resolved it by the end by having the falling words in the final exhibition. It is as though there must be the lack of work for the projection of desire. You need its presence, but out of reach. In the first two exhibitions, the work was too far away for people to really desire it, because there was nothing there for them to project onto, no art, only documentation. So there was too much of a lack really...*

SM You are totally right. This is the wonderful thing about touring exhibitions, of having more than one venue. We were able to develop the idea as we went along. It was Dr. Britton who noticed it first in the *Telephone Repeater Station*. He said the photographs were too beautiful. The Italian photojournalist, Maurizio Cogliandro, with whom we worked, did a wonderful job; he hand-printed all these photographs, absolutely gorgeous. But in a sense they created a veil or screen that the spectator couldn't puncture. There was no point of entry for the work. We filled the space with too much stuff. It is hard to remember to leave a gap. I'm interested in what you said because now I'll try to leave gaps in my talks.

ECp   *I'm interested in the word opposed to the image and how you use both, the way that the word is a signifier, that distances people as it isn't a thing. It is only a signifier. So it's like a veil. When you spoke about turning all the words of your thesis white, then there is even less there also. I think it works well with photographs of those words in the grass because you've got the image, which is so abundantly there, and it is really all at once and it just comes at you. And they are words that you have decoded, which is a kind of blockage and the tension is really nice.*

SM   There is a sense that when you work with non-meaning, it immediately puts the spectator back into play to make meaning from non-meaning.

SK   *During your talk, a remark made by the psychoanalyst Dany Nobus occurred to me: psychoanalysis is like going fishing with a net, but instead of trying to catch the fish, psychoanalysis releases them and investigates the residues. Would you respond to that, as you talked so insistently about residues?*

SM   I don't really understand what I'm doing even though I've written twenty thousand words about my current work. I don't understand why I do it; I don't understand the weird relationship I have with books rather than with reading. I want to rupture the meaning in Freud's *Interpretation of Dreams*. I want to bruise it or rub myself up against it. I want to access his text in a way that is not conventional. It is not only with that project; in *bibliomania* – the booklists from artists – I found that an artist's references were just as interesting as his or her work. In a sense, that's the detritus of the artist because it is not often presented. Usually the finished object, the finished work, is presented, not their reading list. If I had a choice, I'd rather any day Haim Steinbach's reading list than one of his works, although his works are perfectly lovely. His reading list is absolutely fantastic and tells me so much more about him. The psychoanalyst also works with the slippages, the mistakes, the rubbish in the bottom of the net, the clinker or the slag rather than working with what would traditionally be viewed as the interesting products, the objects or deliberate constructions.

SB *I'm interested how you deconstruct and at the same time construct language, not only by cutting it up but also by making it meet the street. Would you expand on your relationship with language?*

SM I'm obsessed by language. Dr. Britton and I made a piece called *Performed Absence*. I was due to give a lecture at the University of Leeds on my practice and he went and performed as me while I sat outside in the car park. Andy Warhol used to do this – the advantage is you can always send someone better looking than yourself. For this performance, Dr. Britton became the signifier of Simon Morris. It was horrendous to watch on video later. He comes in with these huge folders I'd prepared for him and says, 'You poor people, you're lucky you've got me today instead of him because he'd subject you to an avalanche of words. He's got a real problem with language. It's always too much. He doesn't know when to shut up when talking about his art practice.' So these questions are very dangerous.

SB *I don't know your other work, but is it text or language you're obsessed with?*

SM It is always about the text and finding meaning in it. *bibliomania* is a collection of artists' booklists, their references for the books that have informed their practice or influenced them. I did a project called *interpretation*, which is quite an easy one to explain. Sharon Kivland wittily referred to it as 'an academic blind date'. I invited two writers to write a text. They found it very agreeable at first because often writers have to work for a journal, where there are restrictions about what they can talk about and for how long they talk about it, word counts and so on. I said they could write whatever they liked, but it had to have fully referenced footnotes. After having done *bibliomania*, presenting the books from the lists for sale at their normal price in book stores, so instead having a category like Sculpture or History, you had Joseph Kosuth or Cindy Smith – a person became a category and that was the only thing that separated them from the rest of the bookstore, Dr. Britton interviewed me about the project. In our exchange, I was trying to explain the project to him and I said it's like an academic text, with the main body of the text and then the footnotes. Some people don't bother with the footnotes but often the footnotes are the most interesting thing, because academics often have arguments there or say rude things about each other knowing that people don't usually read them, using the footnotes in all sorts of exciting ways. When I read that, I thought that would be a great project – the footnotes give you a mental impression of the text. So I got two writers to write an academic essay, one in London, a fantastic writer called Forbes Morlock and the other in New York, Liz Dalton, another fantastic writer. They both wrote and sent their texts to me. They didn't know each other at all. I erased their texts. I turned the title and their text white. This was my difficult job – the piggy in the middle, tongue firmly in cheek. I then sent the references to the opposite person. They had to reconstruct the other person's text from the references. I was awful actually, a terrible piggy in the middle. All I told Forbes was that Liz had a code and he'd never crack it. He became obsessed; he had to work out what she had written about. She had written about Charles Dickens' *Hard Times*, exchanging the pronouns at the beginning of *Hard Times*, which completely changed the ending. He spent nine months on it, putting the footnotes around the walls of his study and he did crack the code. So that was a project that spun out of *bibliomania*. There is an interest in marginalia, in the residue, not the main text, not the object, but I can't tell you why. I leave that to trained professionals.

TN *Does the uncanny connect Ruscha, Freud and the cigarette packet? How aware were you of the chain of uncanny events, and how does that chain dictate your practice? There are links in* bibliomania *too...*

SM I go back to Sol LeWitt's sentences on conceptual art, following something irrationally, logically all the way through to its final conclusion. There is nothing that connects Ruscha's project with Freud's, apart from that when I was reading Freud, as soon as I saw the words 'royal' and 'road', at that moment I thought of Ruscha's work and I imagined throwing the words out of a car window and wanted to see what it might look like. There is no rational explanation for it. There are uncanny things that happen in the project like the cigarette packet of Royals, but there could have been a packet of Silk Cut or Benson & Hedges, and that would also have worked to a degree.

TN *But how much does this chain of events really affect your work?*

SM The project was founded on that initial moment of recognition. It's not a reading; it's a misreading or misrecognition. It's like rubbing up or bruising Freud's book, rupturing it, breaking its meaning apart by rubbing Ruscha's book against it. There is no reason to do it and the words don't justify the action. It was just something I wanted to do. Once I had the thought, I wanted to follow it through and it finally reached its conclusion when the spectators involved with the ripping and tearing, encounter the aleatory moment.

Audience *You quoted someone saying that language is phallic. Could you expand?*

SM It's probably time to resort to my second prepared answer...You could refer back to Bracha Lichtenberg Ettinger's essay from which the quote was taken.[3] She gives an excellent description of language as phallic and provides a concise reading of Lacan's three registers; the Imaginary, the Symbolic and the Real. I'm not particularly interested in that part of her comment, when she refers to language as phallic but I am interested in what she says about working with marginalia, finding different ways of working with language. It makes me think of Sophie Calle and her *Double Game* and also of Luce Irigaray's ways of approaching text. Are you familiar with Sophie Calle's *Double Game*? The writer Paul Auster heard about Sophie Calle's extraordinary practice and decided to write about her as a fictional person. He asked for her permission, changing her name to 'Maria'. She takes it back because she then did a project called *Double Game*, in which she remade both her own projects and the fake ones, because he made up some extra ones for her. Now the distinction between truth and fiction has been blurred. Calle then sewed some of Paul Auster's original pages from *Leviathan*, his book, into her book, *Double Game*. This provides ways of subverting discourses, of reading from left to right, of putting things together in sentences and paragraphs and structures that we are so used to.

Audience   *Much of your work is quite logical and ordered and has rules about construction or deconstruction. Yet you seem to have a whimsical attitude towards inspiration or ideas. Do you find that is what makes you an artist, the exciting thing about what you do?*

SM   I became aware, working on *The Royal Road to the Unconscious*, of thinking, what is an art work? Where does it exist? John Keats wrote 'that which is created must create itself'. There is a tension in art works between being a very ordered, intentional practice of set procedures and moments that are beyond any control. Both Salvador Dalí, and Max Ernst used to talk about themselves as mediums: the work passed through them, they were just mechanical recording devices. The work came from somewhere else. I used to think art was ordered and programmed and you just did it. I've become more and more aware that there is something else going on. I have no idea what it is. There is an aspect of the irrational and I love the tension between the order and the disorder. As the Dada artists used to say: the yes and the no, they belong together.

1   John Cage, *Silence*, Hanover, New Hampshire: Wesleyan University Press, 1973, pp.109-26.

2   *http://wings.buffalo.edu/epc/authors/goldsmith.*

3   Bracha Lichtenberg Ettinger, 'Matrix and Metramorphosis', in *Differences: A Journal of Feminist Cultural Studies*, 1993, vol.4.3.

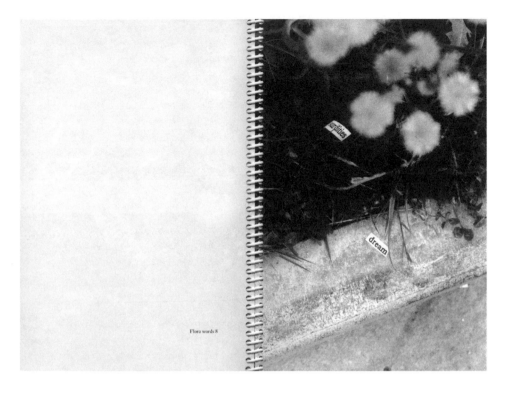

Flora words 8

Victor Burgin

Victor Burgin has exhibited his work internationally over many years, and his photographic and video works are represented in major museum collections worldwide. His theoretical works include *Thinking Photography* (1982), *The End of Art Theory* (1986), *Some Cities* (1996), *Victor Burgin* (2001), *Relocating* (2002), and *The Remembered Film* (2004). He is Millard Professor of Fine Art at Goldsmiths College, University of London and Professor Emeritus of History of Consciousness at the University of California, Santa Cruz.

Victor Burgin took up the wider theme of transmission as much as inscription, beginning with his return to Sheffield, his hometown where his earliest memories lie, on the train. The train journey, between London and Sheffield, departure and arrival, provided the structure of his lecture, as a metaphor for the imposition of definite shape on an abstract continuum, a non-place in the sense of Marc Augé's work, suggesting a contingent, mobile appellation rather than any permanent condition. Drawing on Henri Lefebvre's *The Production of Space* (1974), he moved from notions of spatial practice as perceived and conceived, to spatial practice as lived, that is, representational space that is appropriated by the imagination, with the dimension of fantasy. Burgin suggested that the real city cannot be distinct from its mental representation, and that equally, the railway is a site of objective material invention and an object of desire, the industrial projection of fantasy. He linked the railway with the panoramas of the nineteenth century, as dominant forms of spectator immersion. The train was described as a metaphor for mental processes; a train journey suspending time and the external view in a perpetual state of decomposition. The narratives of the journey by train are close to the narrative structure of dreams, and the space may be appropriated by the imagination. Burgin showed extracts from two video works: in the first, the railway is apparent, while in the second there is latent suggestion of the railway as precipitating cause. The lecture constructed a space of reverie, as a work of train journeys interrupted by trains of association.

Contributors *Dave Beech, Emma Cocker, Charlie Hope, Jaspar Joseph-Lester, Tom Newell, Michael Prince.*
Chair *Sharon Kivland*

DB *I'd like you to talk more about the multiple-screen presentation. There doesn't seem to be a multiplication — we don't get the same thing three times. It's more like a split, like montaging several things together. In which case, is the spectator split or completed by the montage? Are we bringing this together into a comprehensive whole or does the split remain split?*

VB The issues you are raising concern the difference between, on the one hand, working for a theatrical setting, like the one we are in now — that's to say, making 'movies', whether documentaries or fiction films — and, on the other hand, working for the gallery space. I belong to a generation critical of Clement Greenberg and modernist aesthetics, but I have retained from Greenberg the insistence on what he calls the 'specificity' of a practice, that which marks out one practice from other practices. What are the specific conditions of making videos for a gallery setting as opposed to making them to be shown on television, or in a cinema? Spectator position is one of these. In the gallery you have a peripatetic spectator, not fixed in place as in the cinema. In the gallery you can move, and most people do. The work you are referring to was made to occupy three galleries, side by side, and when you were in one room, you could not see the image in the other rooms. Although the image on the screen was identical in each room, there was no way you could simply see that, immediately, without taking the time to work it out. That allows a duplication, and yet at the same time, in terms of the spectator, as you suggest, it is not a duplication. It's a real duplication, but not an imaginary duplication.

Regardless of how many screens are used, you don't know at what point a spectator will enter the space and at what point he or she will leave. Most film and video works made for galleries are made to loop. Some videos shown in galleries have titles at the beginning and, at the end, they roll the credits – just like in the movies. You can do that, but it's not specific to the spectatorial conditions of the gallery space. For example, I am currently adapting an eighteenth-century French novella for the voice-over soundtrack for a new work. At first I thought I simply had to condense the story. But I then I realised that condensation alone was not going to work for me, because the spectator who walks into the work near the end is going to feel that they've got there prematurely. So, for a loop, the story needs to be endless. This story is about a man who seduces a woman by showing her his house. It was first published in 1758 and was commissioned from the writer, Jean-François de Bastide, by an architect. The idea was that the novella would attract clients for the architect. In effect, he was saying to these wealthy men: 'If you have me build and decorate your house you can't fail!' At the end of the story, the virtuous lady succumbs to the charming gentleman, but only because she has first fallen for his house – it's an architectural seduction. In the book, she comes to the house, goes through it room by room, in the last room there's the *dénouement*, and it's over. Roll credits. The book is a suite of descriptions of the rooms, punctuated by exchanges between the two protagonists. In my version, I begin with a description of the garden. The protagonists emerge from this description and the narrative motion begins. At what would have been the end I have her evade him and escape back into the description of the garden. So the story loops without resolution. In this way I was able to restructure a standard linear narrative in a form that was specific to the gallery.

MP *Is it important the work can't be seen as a whole by the viewer at any point, like the view from the train window, a constant stream of images, but you can't see the whole journey? The journey's a series of images, thoughts and recollections.*

VB I assume you're referring to the three-screen work for the Mücsarnok Museum, in Budapest. That was made in 1997, but the interest in making recollection a structural factor in my work is there from the beginning. What characterised the conceptualism of the late 1960s and early 70s was an interest in doing away with material forms of art – we felt there was enough stuff cluttering up the basements of museums. One of the earliest articles written about this – by Lucy Lippard – was called 'The Dematerialization of Art'. You can see how very far removed the original conceptualism was from what gets called 'conceptual art' today. So how do you make art that is somehow both there and not there? One of the first essays I published was in the art magazine *Studio International*, in 1969. I described a work I'd made in Greenwich Park, in London, a couple of years earlier, which consisted of two large triangles, made by stretching ropes flat on the ground. I made one in a hollow near a path by an entrance to the park. Seeing this triangle, you might think, 'They're going to plant something'. And you forget about it and walk on. But if you stay on that path, when you reach the other side of the park, there's another identical rope triangle, and that makes you think of the first one. You might then recapitulate the journey between the two triangles, with associations that would be different for each individual, but the one thing that every viewer would have in common would be that whatever their personal associations, they would coalesce around seeing, then recalling, that rope triangle. The work was called *Memory Piece*. The rope triangle wasn't there to be looked at, as a thing in its own right; it was a cue to trigger a mental event. It was a minimal form of physical presence required to bring this about. The 'object' was not the thing sitting there; it was whatever happened in your head. Every work I've done since has returned to that problem, or 'problematic' – if we define a 'problematic' as a complex of interrelated problems – so I've been circulating through this in various ways, hence the interest in semiotics because that concerns the signifier, the material part of the sign, and in psychoanalytic theory, because that concerns associations in memory and fantasy.

EC *I am interested in the different speeds that operated in the work, particularly the train piece. This was the connection to the panoramas of the nineteenth century to which you referred so extensively. How does that relate to the spatial practices, the perceived, the conceived and the lived, according to Henri Lefebvre? Do they operate at different speeds?*

VB They are different modes of description of the same object – just as this table can be described in terms of 'temperature', 'volume' and 'mass'. Theories don't talk about a pre-existing object: rather, they construct the object. Every discipline needs to have its own object: for example, the object of psychoanalytic theory is the unconscious. Lefebvre's object is space, but how does he conceive of space? How does he want us to think about space? He looks at it through the categories of the 'perceived', the 'conceived' and the 'lived'. The perceived is the empirical – what you actually see, the water jug on the table and everything else. But what tends to be ignored here, right away, are the non-empirical aspects of the perceived. We have the object of perception, but then there is the intellectual schema through which the object is seen. For example, if you were a painter, painting the water jug, then you might see the object through linear perspective, if you've been trained in that tradition. Or you might see it through the schema of Cubist aesthetics, if you have been exposed to that aspect of the history of art. You are looking at the thing in the world through inherited intellectual schemata. This is what Lefebvre means by the 'conceived'. But you're also prey to your own associations, memories and emotions, so there's an imaginary dimension at work, and Lefebvre doesn't really deal with this. By the 'lived' Lefebvre means the broadly sociological aspect of space. But it's never just a matter of defining the Park Hill flats in relation to Sheffield society – it is not only a matter of making clear the articulation between physical realities and the pre-existing intellectual schemata and social relations through which they are viewed, but a matter of the imaginary schemata, which means, ultimately, considering the unconscious.

SK *I'd like to ask about anxiety provoked by the circularity of the work, the looping back. The conclusion of a narrative relieves the anxiety of the spectator. When the narrative doesn't end, isn't resolved – there is anxiety. What does a spectator do with that anxiety? If it doesn't end, do we end?*

VB We end, that's for sure. The entropic body comes to an end. The immortal soul carries on for some, those of us who don't have one are out of luck. Assuming, then, that spectators become anxious (they are equally likely to become angry or frustrated)... Narrative cinema, and other forms of narrative fiction, works through the creation of moments of tension and release towards a final resolution. In the end there'll be the shoot out at the OK corral, a catharsis, and you'll leave, purged of emotion, thoroughly cleansed. In the kind of structure that I'm interested in, you don't get that, though you can leave the gallery to write a nasty review, which is a kind of catharsis. I go back to Donald Winnicott, the idea of the object used by each spectator according to their capacities and inclinations. In particular terms, your question would have to be answered differently in relation to each individual spectator. All you can say about it generally is structural. You're referring to another aspect of the specificity of the loop, as differing from traditional narrative structure in that the tension/resolution pattern achieves no end. I would add that to speak of a loop is not necessarily to speak of repetition. For example, I try to trick the recognition of the point of entry by shifting clues. You may think there's a point you recognize where you came in, but what comes afterwards is something you haven't seen before. It's quite difficult for the spectator to form an idea of the form of the work as a totality. If you were determined to come away with an accurate account of your experience, then it would be different for every person.

JJ-L *Would you say more about the resistance to – or lack of interest in – representational space?*

VB During the 1990s debates about space were prominent on the West Coast, where I was teaching at that time. Edward Soja, at UCLA, was one of the main representatives of spatial enquiry, but in a sociological, statistical way. Soja is explicitly hostile to considering the fantasy dimension of our relation to space. I felt rather isolated at that time, in that place, trying to theorise space in terms of 'psychical space', an idea derived from psychoanalytic theory, which I first put into my article 'Geometry and Abjection', published in AA Files in 1987. I felt there was a considerable resistance to thinking in that way. I wonder if that feeling is now rather out-dated. Probably there is more work now that takes into account the psychical dimension of fantasy. So I was really talking about the state of affairs at the time I published my book *In/Different Spaces*, in 1996.

TN *You said that the rhythmic qualities of the train journey and music played a powerful part in the videos. Would you talk more about the role of music in your work, and the role music plays in memories of our experience?*

VB I am suddenly overcome with humility. Why should I talk about this, rather than anybody else? Isn't music important in the lives of everyone? We have all experienced hearing a tune that take us back to a previous moment in our lives, associated with a good or bad time.

Although you're of a different generation, I would be surprised if you did not have a sense of the historical period of the film music, or of the quality of the language and the actors' voices, on the clip I showed. Time and music are tied together: the 'time of the music' in both the musical and the historical sense. To answer autobiographically, music is terribly important to me. If we return to the context of art, thinking again about the specificity of the works, then you could say, given the physical apparatus of video – with a soundtrack and an image track – there are different registers of spoken words, written words, musical sound, noises, images in black and white or colour, moving or still – that's the specificity of the complex, those are the building bricks. You don't have to use all of them, but with each choice one is beholden to think about consequences. You've got these things you can use, you are free to do anything with them, but you are responsible for what you do. I am free to use music, but I am responsible for what I do. So what are the parameters of that responsibility? First, there is a sense of deference towards music. Even one of the most arrogant of my gods, Jean-Luc Godard, had this deference towards music, saying, 'all images need music, music never needs images'. I try to treat music respectfully, not just as background music. The music is there in its own right. If I'm using music in a video, it becomes a signifier, a means of punctuation, or something else. In Winnicott's terms, I'm involved in the creative use of a found object. In the video *Listen to Britain* I use 1940s film music because, although it doesn't have great merit as a piece of music, it opens up, just as the voices do, the space between the present – between standing on that hill in Kent in the present – and another time. That exchange between the two voices on the soundtrack, laden with a socialist resolve towards the end of the war, a resolve that after the war gave us the first Labour government, that in turn gave me my grammar school education, coming from a working class family in Sheffield. What happened to that version of Britain? The music functions equally as the 'grain of the voice', giving the texture of that history.

In the other piece, the three-screen Sandor Ferenczi piece, music functions differently. There are short bursts from Richard Strauss's opera *Der Rosenkavalier*, the story of a middle-aged woman who has a young man as a lover. By the end of the opera, she has given him up to a young woman. As it's an opera, it takes her three hours to get there. That could be mapped onto the triangle of Ferenczi and the two women – the story I told you – but with the gender roles reversed – it's a story of generational renunciation, as it were. Ferenczi was an opera buff, always trying to get Freud to go to the opera, completely without success. My research showed that there was indeed a performance of *Der Rosenkavalier* in Budapest that Ferenczi almost certainly saw, so that further anchors the choice of music in terms of the story and the historical period. This kind of anchorage is important to me, because I'm in sympathy with Eisenstein when he accused Vertov of 'unmotivated camera mischief'. I don't like unmotivated mischief. I like to feel there is a good foundation. I remember speaking to an architect at a party in California and complimenting him on his house, which had been published in an architectural magazine, He said, 'It breaks my heart, because we are in earthquake country, and two thirds of the budget went into the foundation and you can't even see it!' *(laughs)* The way I work is that two thirds of the effort goes into the foundation, and you don't even see it, but it's necessary to have that firm foundation. Of course that's a way of evading answering the question, what does it mean for you emotionally? You can give an answer, but it can't be an honest answer. As Wittgenstein famously said, 'Everything that can be thought, can be thought clearly, everything that can be said can be said clearly, but not everything that can be thought can be said.'

CH *Is it important your work has a seductive quality? You said you have trouble getting people to commit time to watching work. Do you think it's important to seduce them into paying attention?*

VB I said, rather, that one of the differences between moving image work in the gallery and moving image work in a cinema, is that in the cinema you accept a social convention. You've paid your money, you sit down and then you watch, whereas in the gallery you haven't paid anything, and so are free to say 'hey, what the hell!'; if you're not going to be entertained, you're going to leave. We are living in an entertainment culture, and this is driving a lot of work in the galleries. People expect to be entertained. There's a difference between being seduced and being entertained. I ask you to interrogate your own experience and ask if you were being seduced or merely entertained. To be absolutely honest, and just a bit paranoid – I really am thinking now, 'what's he asking me?', or, 'what's he telling me in his question? Is he telling me this shit bored him? Can't he just say so?' Now I am expressing my anxiety that you would have been bored by this shit. Of course, shit is the child's first offering to the parents, and the question is, 'does the parent love me?' An aspect of what an artist does is to make a gift for another, and the fundamental question is, 'will they accept my gift or will they turn away?' 'Am I loved?' is always the ultimate question. Now it's hard to do 'difficult' work and be loved, let's face it. It's no accident that I wound up spending so much time in France. The Anglophone world prides itself on its pragmatism, its down-to-earth rationality. It's a fiercely anti-intellectual world, as is the art world it contains. In a gallery setting in which people are free to come and go without paying, they nevertheless ask if they're getting their money's worth – because time is money. So how can I put something there that is going to hold the audience's attention? After much thought I have come to the conclusion that it's not worth thinking about. You can't please everybody, so you might as well please yourself. You can't speak of the audience, you can only speak of individuals, and you don't know them as individuals. You can't say anything that has any likelihood of accuracy about the individuals, you can only generalise about them as a crowd. Well... they probably all watch television, they probably all read the British press, so they are probably all brain damaged. But beyond that dumb generality you can't say too much. For me, too much art today is aimed at the crowd. You are free to do anything, but you are responsible for what you do. Your ethical responsibility as an artist is to be irresponsible towards your audience, irresponsible to the normative mass that advertising aims at. You have a responsibility to the truth – not in any universal or transcendental sense, but truth to your own experience. I write, and I make visual work. When I'm doing the visual work I'm trying to say something that I don't know. When I look at what I've made, I ask myself 'Is that what it is?' The reply is, 'Not really, but it's as close as I can get.' It's the disappointment, the recognition of failure, which pushes you into trying to get it right next time. This is to say that the work is difficult for me. I don't want to do something that is without a seductive quality. That is another part of the specificity of art practice, historically – pleasure is part of it. In a psychoanalytic context, there are as many pleasures as there are individuals. As we know, pain can be pleasurable. Difficulty itself can be a form of seduction.

Overleaf:
Victor Burgin
Szerelmes Levelek / Love Letters

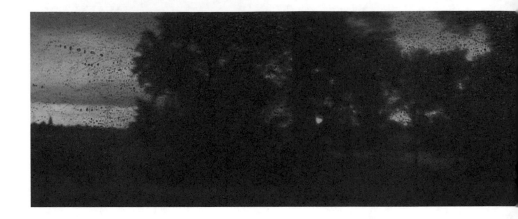

Szerelmes Levelek/Love Letters was commissioned for the Mücsarnok Museum, Budapest, where it was shown in 1997. The work is based on an exchange of letters between Sigmund Freud and the Hungarian psychoanalyst Sándor Ferenczi, one of the earliest and most brilliant of Freud's collaborators. In 1900, eight years before he first met Freud, Ferenczi had begun an illicit affair with a married woman eight years his senior. In the summer of 1911, at the woman's request, Ferenczi took her youngest daughter into analysis. The daughter was then twenty-four years old, Ferenczi was thirty-eight. In the winter of 1911 Ferenczi wrote to Freud to confess that he and the daughter had fallen in love. A long correspondence ensued in which Freud eventually persuaded Ferenczi to give up his relationship with the younger woman. Ferenczi coined the expression 'father transference' to speak of the daughter's feelings for him. The idea of 'transference' emerged at the very beginning of psychoanalytic theory, but its specificity was not brought into focus until the publication of Freud's paper 'Observations on Transference-love'. Freud's essay was published in 1915, there can be little doubt that when he wrote it his exchange with Sándor Ferenczi must have been prominent amongst his thoughts.

In my work for the Mücsarnok I restored these two previously disparate items – Freud's 'dispassionate' scientific paper on psycho-analytic technique, and Ferenczi's letters about the conflict between his emotions and his ethical principles – to their original proximity.

The installation took the form of three large projected video images in three long adjoining galleries that connect in a straight line, like the compartments of a railway carriage. There was much coming and going between Budapest and Vienna in the course of the Ferenczi/mother/daughter affair. What is seen in the video consists mainly of images of the Hungarian countryside shot from the train between Budapest and Vienna. The images are identical in each room, but the sound heard with the images changes as the viewer passes from one room to the next. The sound heard at one extremity of the corridor of galleries is of a voice telling the story of the love triangle from Ferenczi's point of view. The text is based on edited excerpts from his letters to Freud. The sound heard at the other extremity of the sequence of galleries is of a voice speaking a précis of Freud's essay on transference-love. In the central gallery these previously separated monologues come together in a dialogue. In allusion to the otherwise 'silent' figures of the two women the words of Freud are spoken by a mature woman, and those of Ferenczi by a younger woman. Psychoanalysis had flourished in Hungary until Fascism killed or scattered its practitioners. Under the post-war communist regime the practice of psychoanalysis was forbidden. Even today there are few works by Sándor Ferenczi available in his native language. The occasion of my video for the Mücsarnok Museum was the first time any of this particular exchange with Freud had been translated into Hungarian.

Mark Titchner
Por que hay algo en lugar de nada?
2004
Billboard, Mexico City

09.02.05 **Mark Titchner**

Mark Titchner's practice involves graphic texts, sculptures and films that scrutinise the way belief systems function. These works touch on a myriad of scientific, religious and philosophical references that have held particular influence over the last hundred years. Mark Titchner is represented by Vilma Gold; his work has been widely exhibited at international venues which include Tate Britain, The Groninger Museum, Museum Morsbroich, Lehnbachhaus Munich, State Russian Museum and Museo Tamayo. Titchner has also recently written and illustrated a book entitled *Why and Why Not*, published by Book Works, London.

Titchner showed a large selection of text-based work and discussed ways that systems of power and belief are hidden within language. In the video work *Artists are cowards* (2002), a series of words are momentarily projected onto the screen. The processes through which text might appear to work on a subliminal level were discussed in relation to advertising which, if not already animated, was seen to gain the power of movement through its relation to the passing viewer. *Voices you cannot hear tell you what to do* (2004) is similarly concerned with the way that language, in this case Rock music, could contain subliminal messages encoded within it. The homeopathic notion of water recording information was then discussed in relation to work that attempted to make speech visible as Titchner showed documentation of his solo show at the Tate Britain which used an echo chamber and wave patterns to record the visitors' (primal) screams. In each case, the process of making language transparent meant that language inevitably lost its meaning. Titchner explained that the main crux of his digital and text-based work involved the recontextualisation of diverse and varied source material. For the 'Platform for Art' commission, Titchner took material from trades-union banners and multinational corporation manifestos. From this, and other source material, a series of ten posters were made for Gloucester Road underground station. Empty slogans such as 'We Want...' could be read as a series of demands or, as Titchner put it, an 'inversion of the Ten Commandments'. He discussed the power dynamic inscribed within the English language and his interest in revealing the ideological imperatives that language embodies.

Contributors *Emma Cocker, Tom Newell*
Chair *Jaspar Joseph-Lester*

TN *In this sort of situation you've got the opportunity to spell certain things out to us but how do you feel about not being able to explain your work in the gallery environment?*

MT This is an extremely unusual situation and it's actually quite misleading. I write about the work as well so there's that aspect of it but much of the work is visually overloaded. When talking about text and reading, the experience of being in front of a work, going through the process of trying to put it together, to work out what it is, is crucial. I use repeated motifs within the work as well. I didn't show you all of what

I do but I've been using certain elements repeatedly to breed some sort of familiarity. The key thing is reading. The texts are straight-forward. I try to use text that doesn't use complicated language. It might describe complicated ideas but the point of engagement is direct. I didn't talk about sculptural works but these, like the work at the Tate, actually require interaction in order to work, whether it's shouting into them or holding on to them. There is consideration of the importance of the viewer. You have to work to put it together. You either lose people or you don't, so you try and grab their attention fairly quickly. The project at Gloucester Road was interesting because you are fighting advertising, and advertising works to grab your attention now, we don't have enough time. That really taught me a lot. You have to hit a fundamental nerve either with text or image to get people to stay and read it because the environment is so filled with text and images anyway. That's why I was interested in working on a television project. In public projects you enter a dialogue that isn't about being in an art gallery.

JJ-L   *I was struck by the incredible fullness and emptiness that co-exist in the work, something that we don't always engage with when we are faced with signs and slogans in everyday life. In this paradoxical excess and emptiness there's something ghost-like, things from the past are kept at a distance and appear to have lost the presence or meaning that they once held. Is it this distance from the complexities of the major political and cultural events, from those things that have moulded the twentieth century, this distance from the past that allows you to reduce the momentous or seminal down to a single statement or image?*

MT   I haven't lived through those times. If we are a product of our past, how do we experience that past? Do we accept it? It's not just about reporting, it's about placement; it's about semiotics. We receive this idea about what our history is and where it starts, what's important, what's not. It's not arbitrary – it's constructed in that way for a certain reason. I would love to walk down the street tomorrow and get this revelation and everything will be fine, but it hasn't happened so what I do is about looking for something. The older I get and the more work I make, the less I understand. I was talking about the problem with the book: with writing you are able, fairly quickly and directly to explain and explore your position and therefore to understand aspects of how your psychology works but in an object you have other less distinct parameters that come into play which are about physically engaging with the audience and there's some solace to be found there in the phenomena of matter rather than in pure ideas. Text is hard and there's nothing else that works so directly. Most of us listen to music –

we are constantly absorbing the melody or the song, absorbing the text. Songs become like weird mantras for people's lives, sound tracks to this movie you're living.

JJ-L *You have discussed how the notion of recontextualization is important in your work. When seen in the space of a gallery or as a work outside the gallery, the slogans that we identify with political banners, advertising and corporate manifestos appear generic. In your work it is as if they become empty signifiers, as if the text operates as a vessel that can be filled with any number of ideologies or systems of belief. Do you think that your work makes visible a certain lack? Through this process of recontextualization, do your works demonstrate the way a specific context determines the meaning of a text?*

MT There are two different things going on. For me, the most interesting works are those where I get the opportunity to work outside galleries. Most successful from my point of view was the Gloucester Road project, whose context determined a face-off between my work and the advertising it confronted. In a gallery, you don't have that moment of questioning.

JJ-L *The relationship with text or images, with things that you already know, is recontextualised in your work. Does this strategy make those things appear the same that really represent quite extreme differences? Different ideologies or systems of belief suddenly become signs, which can be filled with anything.*

MT This was the premise of the light box works, in which I was trying to describe a state in which you don't have any strong beliefs about anything and so you seek them out in the things around you. There is a vacuum of belief or ideology; anything can fill it. The works used philosophical texts or scientific theory, lyrics from a pop song or lines from cheap novels. I wanted these images together. The first one I made said 'Why is there something instead of nothing?', which is the first question of philosophy. It was also the title of a lecture given by Heidegger but it came to me via a song by a band called Silver Jews.

JJ-L *Heidegger came second?*

MT I didn't even know about it until someone else mentioned it to me, but if you were going to ask any sort of question about the universe, that's the question that you ask. If you believe nothing, everything has value.

JJ-L *There is that other piece with two figures, two posters, both with a silhouette of a man?*

MT Yes, it's 'behold the man, waiting for the man', a diptych. 'Behold the man' is from the Bible but bound up with Nietzsche's last blast, as it were, and then 'waiting for the man' is the Velvet Underground song about scoring heroin. It is about a space in between, waiting, but waiting for anything.

JJ-L *We have that experience of the work – a sudden realization of meaninglessness, that signs around us are filled with momentary things, based on context rather than any fundamental essence.*

MT Someone asked me recently, about these particular works, what exactly it is that I do. What I do is de-contextualize them. In some ways it could be seen as an irreverent practice, which it isn't intended to be. The worrying thing is the endlessness of it all, the drive that you have when you're younger, you know, 'kill daddy'. I want to render everything meaningless, but that becomes rather depressing. These strategies are not great to live by; making everything equivalent, you need things that are important.

I was thinking about how the Pope was responsible partly for the collapse of the Soviet Union, as if it wasn't another ideology that just came in and filled its place with Catholicism, as if one ideology was neutral and good and the other was bad. There's an impossibility of standing back completely, seeing everything as a system of different beliefs that can be filled with things that, as you suggest, are similar.

My drive is to try to work out why I don't feel more strongly about certain things, how I justify a moral stance, I still have that feeling when I wake up in the morning that I could go and do something useful today and instead I'm involved in art production! It's a strange thing and morally, not always easy to defend. There's an anecdote about William Burroughs, whose work is about control and possession and power (those are things that I'm interested in), as a child being taken into the woods by a nanny who was into witchcraft and a spirit possessed him. He was obsessed by what controlled him and what stopped it and that's something that I identify with. Sometimes I don't understand why I do things; it doesn't make sense. I don't feel strongly about things in the way that I feel I should do.

JJ-L *But you're drawn at the same time to do something particular?*

MT I think and deal in extremes. If I did feel that way, then I would be trying to do something about it, rather than dealing with abstract problems. I navigate my way through the passages. When certain people see the work, they know it's mine, and that effects how they read it, which is a different problem, setting up a certain aesthetic. That relates to that question of what it is that I do exactly.

JJ-L *You already rely on being recognized, being memorable in terms of image or text.*

MT I'm happy to continue because their excess drives home the point. But recently I've begun investigating methods where text is used in a way that it is not recognizable as text. I've been working with coding and also I'm looking at occult practices that use text as an entry point and that's to do with use and interaction. I did set out by saying I'm only going to work in English and Esperanto, but I've been in situations where the rule doesn't hold. Working in Wales, putting up a huge English banner obviously has connotations so I worked with the Welsh Assembly to translate these texts in to Welsh, which represents more than the purely linguistic. That context for me is interesting, and I am working on some pieces in Spanish. Sometimes I think it's – not a sell out – but a loosening of ideals. It opens things up rather than closes them down, though.

EC   *I am interested in the way that you describe the work as emptied out of meaning. Must the empty message retain residue in order for the contrast to work, for example the contrast between the Velvet Underground lyrics and the text from the Bible? You talk about hiding behind something in the work, and in particular in your decision to return to sculpture in order to hide behind form or the technical difficulties of making. Can you talk more about what you are hiding in the work, or indeed what you are hiding from?*

MT   What I was talking about was to do with my book. Part of the interesting and the difficult thing about writing is the ability to state something clearly and simply in a short period of time. I found that when I was working on the book that I was able to empty out what I felt about things, my beliefs and hopes, very quickly. That's a scary thing and I had to set up an extreme working situation in order to move away from that. The three months that I was working on the book were crazy. The first part of it I wrote when I was in Mexico and I had jet lag so I was awake all the time. I was writing at night and I found that it helped to loosen my brain up. When I got home, I started waking myself up in the middle of the night and writing, which is unpleasant but very effective.

JJ-L   *What was the effect?*

MT   Well, it's that writer's block thing, sitting at a desk staring at a blank page thinking what do I do. When you wake up in the middle of the night, you've broken into a dream and your consciousness is slightly unbalanced. I'd try to fill the whole day with writing at night, reading on the way in, doing some more research. It allowed me to not get too tied down with individual ideas. The premise for that book was the fluidity with which you can move between contradictory ideologies. Formal problems never go away, they're always going to be there and they're actually more enjoyable to deal with than some fundamental question that you know that deep down you know you'll never answer (all you can do is assume a relative position). I do talk about hiding but that's probably fairly extreme language... staring into the abyss, you naturally have an inclination to stay away from it. Much of this editing process is to do with that; I suppose it's a nihilistic procedure.

EC *There is a strange cancelling out in your work, which seems to come from the tension between overstating the visual element of the word and understating the reference.*

MT The only thing that I would add to that is that there's no point in the work where you're told where the reference material comes from, so that voice is always invisible, the voice of the author disappears.

EC *Can you talk more about coding within your work, about the layered references and how an audience might approach this? Do you require a knowing viewer who is able to identify your references?*

MT Coding is important as it relates to understanding. What happens is that a certain belief or message becomes coded to the point where it becomes an aesthetic, so I think there's a parallel between that and the use of typography in the work. But I'm also interested in what is it possible to know anyway, so by making something unknowable by a simple coding procedure... I am more interested in hiding meaning and trying to use subconscious rather than conscious procedures for the way that text is absorbed, driving it to the point were it becomes illegible as normal text. It becomes something else, a sign for the text, as it were.

Audience *Derrida talks about relations in inscription. He says that there's a moving away from the origin, as if the signifier returns. I think he's talking about the inscription, not as supplement, but as a thing in itself, how a thing is understood. In a traditional sense, inscription stands in for meaning and location.*

MT Any process of mark–making or writing or speech moves away from the original figures and becomes representation, and so your understanding of those figures changes. The piece at the Tate is like a primal scream, trying to reduce language to a fundamental point of creation, the first word or the birth scream, simplifying it as the first inscription, the point at which the world changed forever. Burroughs talked about the word as a virus, lodged in the throat.

JJ-L *As poster images, their 'surface-ness' allows for a different level of engagement – you then project your own meaning onto that empty vessel.*

MT The whole point is that the projection is of a desire and to do it in a way that means that you don't actually realize that you're doing it.

JJ-L *What you're doing is making that visible.*

MT   That's the idea; the problem is that these are things between things, they're fine points that are difficult to communicate. It's part of what I do; in order to make a point I have to be very ham-fisted sometimes. It's that Duchamp thing of the sound of the man wearing velvet trousers walking down the street, it's the spaces between and the tiny hole and that's where things begin to unravel.

JJ-L   *You use technology in the generation of voice within the work, to create machine-generated sound. What is the significance of this?*

MT   *The voices you cannot hear* video is about finding an audio equivalent of the text that I used. The text is about (a) something that is incredibly clear and (b) has an authority to it and the use of those computer-generated voices is to make them generic but by being generic man and generic woman, they don't necessarily have any context. They have a ghostly power to them. There's something about not really knowing... disembodied voices, the voice at the airport is telling you where to go or at a station... and you respond to it.

EC   *You seem to suggest that technology has the capacity to offer immediacy but without always making sense. There seems to be an interest in those moments when sense collapses or is unreadable – corrupted files, mistranslations, obsolete programming languages. Is this a dystopian view of the future through technology?*

MT   One of the things that I'm working on at the moment are symbolic wishing machines which are about trying to get the machine to make something happen, which a machine couldn't possibly do. It's about making technology god-like and about that desire. That's a real modernist belief, the belief in technology, in pharmaceuticals and in capital. It's one of the defining characteristics of the Western world: if we have a problem, we look to technology.

EC   *How arbitrary is the process of working with found text. Do you look for certain references or are you interested in certain types of source material?*

MT   Recently I've been working with last words that people said before they died! I've been looking at those of people who were interested in more extreme ideas of manipulating consciousness, so like Timothy Leary, Aldous Huxley, Terrence McKenna, either the last written words or the last words spoken; sometimes it's last audio recordings, last appearances... it also relates to the question of a point at which you understand.

Opposite:
Mark Titchner
We want healthy dissatisfaction
2004
Digital print on aluminium
239cm x 293.5 cm

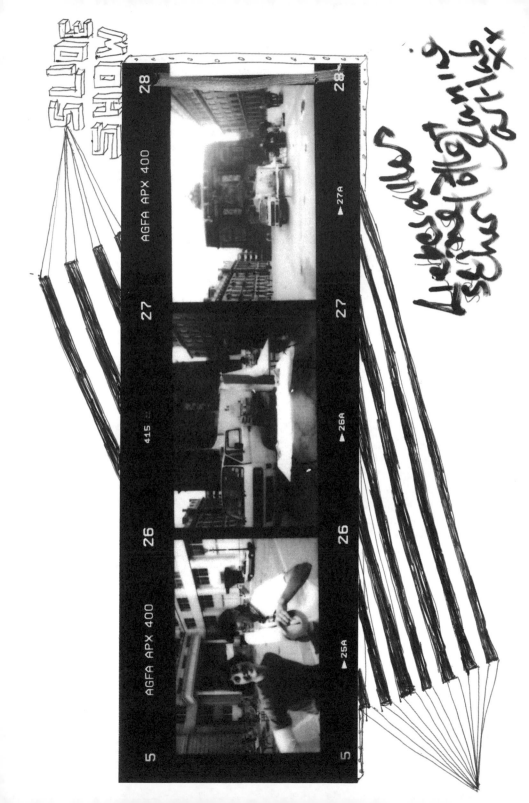

ArtLab C. Cullinan + J. Richards

ArtLab is Charlotte Cullinan and Jeanine Richards. Their practice has included painting, sculpture, cinema, curating, drawing, installation and video. Since their inception in 1998 they have exhibited widely in the UK and internationally, including solo shows at Mobile Home, inIVA and MOT (London). They have been included in numerous group shows including 'Documentary Creations', Kunstmuseum, Luzern, 'Britannia Works', Athens (British Council) and 'Edge of the Real', The Whitechapel Gallery, London.

For their presentation ArtLab showed part of one of their road movies *This is Mayday* (40 mins. 2002) and a work called *Slide Show*. The audience entered the cinema as the film was playing and shortly after this a statement was read out, explaining that the slides that were about to be shown had been found, thrown out, on Vyner Street (London, E2) outside the artists' studio. A large selection of slides then followed, which included images of disused petrol stations, indecipherable diagrams, temporary structures, plans for temporary structures, anarchist artists, architectural details, guns, cars, sculptures and drawings, all of which was shown accompanied by a selection of music from film soundtracks chosen by ArtLab. *Slide Show* is arranged with Jeanine Richards reading out the short statement and Charlotte Cullinan operating the slides and sound from the projection room.

Contributors   *Emma Cocker, Hester Reeve, Dolly Ryall*
Chair   *Jaspar Joseph-Lester*

JJ-L   *John Slyce writes about your work: 'ArtLab deploys an outpost aesthetic in the constructions and seemingly improvisational display of structures, sculptures and paintings. This is a functional aesthetic, perhaps more native to the frontier than to the halls of culture. Everything one needs is there and made to order according to the immediate demands of place, time and setting and primarily from what is close at hand.' Would you care to comment on this — perhaps about the unpredictable nature of your practice as an aesthetic?*

ArtLab   We are interested in use and in context, not necessarily being given a context, but making a context. We like to re-use work, reinventing the reason why it was made. We were trying to address that with our slide show. Some artists don't have much material output; we are the opposite. We are constantly making stuff and that can get depressing.

JJ-L   *You said the slides were found — would you say more?*

ArtLab   When we started working together, we didn't have any shows, so we got big pieces of paper and drew the plans of galleries where we fancied having a show. We then made miniature works and planned the shows. Using what we've got is a fundamental part of what our work's about, an idea of stuff being not worth anything unless it's got a place, a specific (I think that's what the art world is all about) delicately interlocking context. If these slides were being thrown away, you might start to look at them differently. What are all these slides for? What does all that output mean? All those years that we've been working on all these shows and making all this stuff...

JJ-L   *And they could just have been found on the street?*

ArtLab   What if someone did find them in the street? What would they think? Perhaps it wasn't even obvious that it's supposed to be art.

Audience   *On some of the slides, it said ArtLab, didn't it? Is that why you're called ArtLab?*

ArtLab   That's a brilliant question. It is now! We told the story of how the slides were found. We wanted everyone to think about the idea of value and of what art can do, where it's situated, but the slides actually do belong to us. Most of our work is an in-between space of what the audience or visitor is allowed to think about something. So we offer works that include different kinds of art making, but we also offer the space of interpretation of the work. Today we didn't come to do a talk, but to give you a piece of our work – which is what you have just seen. Do you understand that? You've given us a very nice viewpoint, actually.

Audience   *You're not tricking people?*

ArtLab   I don't think so.

JJ-L   *Do you think you're being tricked?*

Audience   *Yes!*

DR   *Why have so many repetitions of the same works?*

ArtLab   There is one for each of us. We have an odd slide collection. You always make connections between one slide and another and so seeing one piece in-between two different slides is interesting. Often works reappear for us in different situations. We're constantly re using stuff. Seeing slides repeated in a different series is another way of doing that.

DR   *It was a shame that I couldn't see what was in the image. Is that a choice or is it poor projection?*

ArtLab   The projection could have been bigger, it could have been in focus, but some of the slides are bad. We don't purposely take crap slides, but if that's the slide that we have, it is better to show it than not.

EC   *Is the inclusion of certain images a strategy to evoke earlier artistic practices? Particularly the images of mannequins, window reflections and the edges of cities, which remind me of images in early Surrealist photography. Is your work inscribed by earlier practices?*

ArtLab   Definitely! We like to plunder whatever we fancy and those are areas that we are very interested in. We are also like being hard to place. Hence we presented these slides the way we did, so that you are not entirely sure about what era these are from.

EC   *There are many images that recur: the petrol station, guns, fashion and outmoded things. From the way that the slides are ordered, do you hope that an audience might excavate the thematic concerns in your practice?*

ArtLab   There was a time when we saw the empty petrol station as a gallery. That is why you see this image more than once. Interpretation of a space or a thing in a space is why we show the slides that we show. The plundering of art history makes us laugh. We do it with our work as well; we take a piece we made and call it something else or use it in a different way. Nothing is sacred.

Audience   *Would you say more about the soundtrack, which appears embedded with the idea of re-use from film or a narrative context implying a new narrative in the visual material?*

ArtLab   We are proposing situations. Within many of the pieces, there is the idea of providing a platform for something to happen or where something may have happened. Works are often based on the idea of an event or a situation that we connect to the idea of the cinematic scenario. We use songs from films randomly, films or songs we like. They are not carefully chosen, but the general idea that the songs have been used in films and then re-used here and this is another level as you're looking at the images. We invited the technician, Dave, to choose one. It's not as careful as you might think.

Audience   *When you say you use what you've got, what do you mean by that? Is the music with the slides like an everyday music we hear now? Do you look for something special?*

ArtLab   No, because obviously we haven't made that music. When we are making pieces, what I mean by the re-use of things is things that we have made ourselves: the products; the sculptures, the paintings, the photographs, the films, we re-use it constantly unless we sell it.

Audience   *So the music is just for now, for the lecture?*

ArtLab   The music is overlaid from other film soundtracks. But the film that was showing when you entered had a soundtrack that was written by an artist called Kev Rice especially for that film, for us. For the slide piece we took songs from films and placed them on top of the slides, so there might be an idea of the film. You know how some songs make you think of particular films? That was the idea.

HR   *You asked 'what is all this for?' That seems to be at the core not only of your practice, but also of many artists' practices, past and present. Your ideas of re-titling and recycling and presenting a petrol station as a gallery, I find very exciting, yet the slides wouldn't help someone who doesn't know your work see it as a gallery. Your work also ends up presenting the reasons for the question you ask. In what way — when artists ask an important question like that —*

should the art practice itself be an answer? Or should it avoid an answer?

ArtLab I don't think we can provide an answer. What we have done works for us. What we have constructed works for the work. There is a self-generated use and meaning for us in the practice. It's self-sufficient. We need a context and we make one. It's a self-contained structure with complexities that relate to other situations, but we are despots in own regime. What we say goes in our practice and that is what we felt we had to do; to take a pathetic control over a pathetic little area. And we are having fun.

HR *Maybe that's more creative than thinking you can answer, which would perhaps close the whole debate?*

ArtLab It means we can think about tomorrow, rather than get blocked.

JJ-L *What kind of context have you created for your practice?*

ArtLab Many of the first pieces we made were simplistic in the sense that they were about situations that didn't rely on the gallery walls. We would make something where we could hang the work, light the work, look at the work and that was the work without using anything from the space around it. We didn't need anything.

JJ-L *You also make a context to show other peoples work as well.*

ArtLab It gets a bit lonely so you need to get someone in there to shake it all up. We offered a situation in our project at Imperial College, constructing a platform for other artists.

EC *Is there is a tension between your practice and its relation to a more conventional gallery practice or the arts sector in a wider sense. Your practice demands a certain amount of self-sufficiency. Does that prohibit you from getting involved in that wider debate?*

ArtLab I don't think so. There are people whose work is parallel to ours, like Thomas Hirschhorn, Karen Klimnick, Martin Kippenberger, Fischli and Weiss…

Audience *How do you work together?*

ArtLab We've worked together since 1998 and I couldn't really work with anyone else. It is easier to be two artists, but it is also harder. People are hung up on who exactly made which bit. We reply, 'sorry, that's none of your business'…

… It's also something to hide behind. It's ArtLab, the two of us. We've just been to Cyprus to look at a site for an exhibition and there was some kind of social hitch and it was 'ArtLab were supposed to phone' and as ArtLab is either her or me, it can be quite a good thing…

… if things go wrong it wasn't me…

… it wasn't me. We swap roles…

… sometimes we do a good cop, bad cop in difficult situations. When you're in a big show there can be quite a bit of posturing and emotional argy-bargy going on. You have to negotiate and fight your corner and it does really help to be two. You can discuss things and not freak out as well...

...You can edit each other. You can start with an idea and sort it out...

... we don't really argue.

... anymore!

JJ-L   *Perhaps more explanation is needed about the way you used the slides?*

ArtLab   It would be nice if you would see it as an art work, rather than a lecture. Most of our work is, it is open to interpretation, so I am not sure if I can say much more.

Audience   *Do you have a finite number of times you re-use a work? Do you worry about it losing something by its re-invention? If you've created it for a purpose, do you consider that it may lose its focus by re-using it repeatedly?*

ArtLab   No, not at all. It gains, actually. There are usually other people involved. If we are making a show that might include particular works of art from the studio and they get reconfigured, there are usually other people between that and the end result; the curator for example.

Audience   *You seem quite apologetic about the poor quality of the slides...*

ArtLab   We are quite proud of that, to be honest.

Audience   *But you keep saying, 'oh, I'm sorry that the lighting was bad' and so on!*

ArtLab   Only because someone else mentioned it. We are unapologetic. That is how we see our work. It isn't perfect; not the commodity product that you imagine art works to be. That is reflected in the slides – the way we make and see our work. It is okay to show crap slides...

... I would have liked the slides to be bigger and in focus, but as to the lighting, when we say that they are not well-lit, we are not apologising. We don't feel bad about that.

EC   *I'm intrigued by your decision to present a slide show in the context of an artist talk series, presenting a work rather than talking about your practice. How is individual work inscribed by the practice of artists? Is there is a difficulty in approaching single works without the context of the artist's wider practice? Why did you decide to present an art work without a context? There is a deliberate sense of not allowing context to be read in relation to the other concerns of your work.*

ArtLab   It does have a context. It has the context of this lecture series, which is specific, carefully constructed. It's in the context of 'Inscription'. It's after a lecture and slide show by Mark Titchner and before another by Lucy Harrison. It's here in Sheffield and we were invited. We're not presenting a piece of work without context. That is what happens when you present slides and say this was a piece we made in Serbia and this was a piece we made in... that then drains its specificity. This is the piece of work in the way we want it to be and you are here and seeing it. For us, that's perfect.

EC   *When I say the context is disallowed I am talking about your artistic practice.*

ArtLab   That's why I told the story at the beginning, because if we had just shown the slides and the music, it's a bit free-fall. What we wanted to do was to create a scenario in which to watch the slides and listen to the music.

EC   *This is a scenario where there is a lead-up by the context of the lecture series to bring up certain issues that you bring to the work. How does that happen when you show in a wider context?*

ArtLab   It's particular to the situation. We have just been to Cyprus on a site visit, trying to develop a piece in response. Sometimes we don't see the site – we are sent a plan or told about a place we can't see until we get there. It is more remote, more about a trusting relationship with a curator who knows the work and us, and technicians who can interpret drawings that are quite vague sometimes. There is a reliance on a team of people and their collaboration, especially if we can't be there. We have never been in a situation when we've arrived somewhere and it's wrong and has to be redone. We don't work like that. It's a gentle process and sometimes things are very different when we get there, but we work with it...

... it's about breaking down hierarchies, not the artist as autonomous commodity-maker. There's so much between the art and exhibition· the curator, the technicians and everyone else one works with.

Audience   *I am interested in your self-satisfaction. I don't know if you feel any artistic progression in re-using the same images in different contexts. You said that you felt it was depressing; don't you feel you are losing something? I was thinking about the artistic progression that I need to feel satisfied, but I don't see it in your work and I wouldn't find it myself in constantly re-using the same images.*

ArtLab   We are constantly making new stuff.

Audience   *What do you gain from re-using a work if you change the context? I know that other people can interpret it differently, but as artists, what do you get from it?*

ArtLab   The same thing as making new pieces. We are very self-satisfied as you can see.

Audience   *The use of found objects, because there is so much cultural production, is interesting, but I'm much more interested in thematising my work and I can't see that in yours. How do you make decisions about whether it's right or wrong to do one thing or another? What is the point; where is something for the audience to grasp, instead of a constant question about the status of an object? What's the meaning of it? How is it useful? How do you choose which objects to present?*

ArtLab   For a show at the Whitechapel Art Gallery last year we made a group of paintings out of paintings that had been seen in other contexts, configured in a certain way that had never been configured before. That – for us – is exciting. It's a re-configuration of paintings, through the curator's eye of studio-based production...

... the curator chose these paintings because they related to performance aspects of our work, the idea of using events, taking those moments and making them into paintings.

Opposite:
ArtLab C. Cullinan + J. Richards
Chandelier for Fascist HQ
2005

Opposite:
Lucy Harrison
Guided Tour (Riga)
2005
Digital print
One from a series of 46, each 25.4 x 20.3 cm

Lenin Museum on Cesu Street

The museum is equipped with an intercom
which plays Lenin's favourite tunes.

Old gramophone recordings
enable one to hear his voice.

23.02.05 Lucy Harrison

Lucy Harrison's work uses collections of texts or information that have been forgotten or ignored. Since leaving the Royal College of Art in 1999, she has lived in East London, where she rents a librarian's office as a studio. Recent projects include *Fantastic Cities* (2004), a book for which twenty-five invited artists wrote about cities they had never visited. Recent exhibitions include 'After the Fact', Tullie House Museum & Art Gallery, Carlisle, *Carpet Slippers No Protection*, George Rodger Gallery, Maidstone, and 'Budget Bureau for language and applications', Centre d'art contemporain, Geneva. She is a lecturer at the Kent Institute of Art and Design, Canterbury.

Lucy Harrison began with a reference to Thomas Bernhard's novel *The Loser*, in which speech is remembered and reported by others. She described her dominant concerns as discarded words, systems of categorization and unreliable reports of the city. Citing her interest in multiples, especially the influence of Ed Ruscha, she traced a chronology through a number of works, from book works to installations, all addressing the subversion of taxonomic systems, the attention to gaps in speech and language, questioning the reliability of speaker, writer and indeed, reader. She presented her book *Good Quote* (2003), a collection of marginalia from the library of Kent Institute of Art and Design, which became a video of students reading out the margin notes as a lecture, and her re-categorization of the Family Sagas section of Sunderland City Library, a work commissioned by the Northern Gallery for Contemporary Art in 2004, which provides an index of an over-specific nature, of emotions and events in the books. Harrison then described a number of works that take the city as a collection of texts, linked by psycho-geographical connections, taking up the subjective nature of urban experience. In her tour of Riga using a Soviet era guidebook, Harrison provides a guide to a city that no longer exists, suggesting, after Michel de Certeau, that reading should not be equated with passivity, that reading modifies its subject and the reader invents in reading, just as lived space is also the space of fantasy.

Contributors *Natalie Allistone, Christine Arnold, Dave Beech, Sylvia Brandstetter, John Clark, Emma Cocker, Chris Gibson, Judy Hockley, Miranda Laughlin, Leah Southwell-Wright*

Chair *Sharon Kivland*

SK *I like the way you left us with the idea of reading as an action, that as readers, we are agents. Your talk connected to Simon Morris's, and to Victor Burgin's; who referred extensively to Henri Lefebvre's* The Production of Space, *most particularly to Lefebvre's idea of lived space. The real space of the city is always attached to a fantasy as you addressed. One of my views of Paris is through a friend, an old soixante-huitard Maoist. In traversing the streets, he describes the city in a nostalgic reconstruction of the events of 1968, the barricades behind which student and workers fought the police and so on. He still lives in his revolutionary city.*

LH Yes, that's an important part of my ideas surrounding cities, most obviously in *Fantastic Cities*, where the contributors relied only on information from sources other than direct experience. Also in the book *Detour*, Christiane Baumgartner and I were documenting our walks in Tallinn, it was also based on previous events from those places. This is why we decided to include the text at the bottom of the pages, like footnotes, because these memories were intruding on what we were trying to do, what we were trying to document. For Christiane, it was a much older memory of having visited as a student during the Soviet era and for me, it was from visits made over the previous two years.

SK *The social geographer, Steve Pile, has a book coming out on ghosts and cities. He proposes that through haunting, the figure of the ghost shows the unpalatable aspects of society. For example, in New Orleans the ghost tour is a way of implicitly speaking about slavery. The haunting is by the dispossessed, the people who are left out of history, who are marginalized.*

LH That reminds me of Peter Ackroyd's book on the Limehouse golem, where the figure from the Jewish legend is re-invented in order to re-direct the blame for a series of murders.

ML *You described your relation with the shop names as romantic and it led me to wonder more about the relations you have with the words you've found and the things you collect. On one hand, you describe the words as misunderstood, forgotten, unwanted and borrowed. On the other, you say they're unreliable, stolen and stupid.*

LH There are different aspects to the different collections and often I try to invert the suggested importance, so I take what other people may see as unwanted and present it as if it had some authority, while at the same time asking whether the published, accepted texts are in fact any more reliable. We are told which texts are important and which aren't, and I try and ignore those categorizations. For instance, I try to give more status to those that have previously been ignored, like the notes in the margins of library books, because if they are still texts, I don't see any reason why they should be swept aside. If something is said in a lecture that is supposed to be left out, I'm being stubborn in including it as important, while the texts that are supposedly 'reliable' can sometimes be shown to be meaningless.

Audience *Would you say more about the typography you use?*

LH It's often a borrowing of a style; I choose a style for the book that indicates how I want it to be viewed. So for example the marginalia are presented with a serif font that is similar to that used in many of the academic books I was using, while *Fantastic Cities* and *Detour* are partly copied from existing guidebooks.

CG *Have you gone back to your* Family Sagas *project in Sunderland Library to find out if it has modified people's reading habits?*

LH I haven't been back, but when the project was on, people from the library often came upstairs to look at the exhibitions anyway; so when they came up to see mine, they were completely confused. It is so arbitrary; the titles I've used are so ridiculous, that it's unlikely that someone will want to use them, even though I did give an A4 version to the library just in case.

SK *In what way could it be used? Would a person want a story of a child abandoned? It would have be someone who thought in categorical terms, and could that only be you?*

LH Perhaps yes – they would have to be in keeping with my own idiosyncratic rules; an extreme version of the subjectivity you always find to a certain extent in systems of categorization.

JH *I heard on the radio that doctors are starting to prescribe books to patients. Also in relation to the* Family Sagas *project, they are talking now about having digital library cards, so that you would end up having lists of the books that people read. Do you have any thoughts on the politics of that?*

LH I suppose it might change how people feel when they're taking books out, knowing that they will be adding to the list of their borrowed items on a computer. Maybe it would stop people making notes in them, knowing that they would be recorded in that way. The prescribing books idea: I haven't heard about that. It would be interesting to prescribe the wrong book and see what people would make of it.

SK *What happens if you fail to find notes? We trust you that these were written in the margins.*

LH Perhaps the book produced in that case would have to be blank – it's important to stick to the rules you give yourself. It would be impossible to rewrite imaginary examples of those notes; they are too strange and fragmentary to make up.

EC *Do you differentiate between the processes of collecting and searching?*

LH I'm not sure if I've made that distinction in the work. With some of the work, like the names on buildings, it's a fairly arbitrary collection that happens as I am doing other things. I see these every day and they become part of what I think about my life in the city. At other times when I've decided what I'm looking for I suppose it does become more of a search, an attempt to complete the overall collection.

EC *Does it connect to night-walking, trying to introduce strategies to enable that aimless practice?*

LH   It is often a strategy of using other people's rules even though I know they are not going to work, so the result is an aimless wander to places no-one else has been to for years.

SB   *When you collect words and phrases, you collect and make a new text out of them. Do you also think of what the form is as a new creation, for example, which words are next to each other, because that could change the meaning? Do you look at them individually or in isolation?*

LH   Yes, it is important that it makes this new piece of writing. Obviously the words in *Good Quote* are in separate places; there could be a few books between them, or a book may have been borrowed or in the wrong place. One day I happen to be looking at that shelf and that puts them together and so it creates this new text. It is complete nonsense, yet at the same time you know these things which didn't go together are answering each other.

LS-W   *What first attracted you to working with text and why do you feel compelled to rescue text? Do you feel it's your responsibility to rescue it?*

LH   As a student I went on exchange to Bilbao, where two languages are spoken. When I came back I found I was listening carefully to people even when they were speaking English. I started writing things down and gradually that led to an interest in words and the different ways you might encounter them. As for responsibility, that is how I felt about the lecture in a way; everyone was writing the same notes, the only record was the script that he was reading from. All these other things were being ignored. I liked the idea that I could take care of these words if no one else was going to.

DB   *In* The Ticklish Subject, *Slavoj Žižek says the universal shouldn't be derived from the hegemonic class, from the official voices of power, but rather from what he calls the 'point of the exception'. The example he gives is single mothers, because they end up carrying the hopes of everyone. This made me think about the way you described the 'errs' in speech. You said they were the one thing that was universal. In my understanding of Žižek, there are two kinds of affective economy going on. Do you see this in your work? There is a tenderness towards the point of exception, but also a sense of violation. There was a hint of that when you talked about how Jonathan Miles was disturbed by your rendering of his lecture.*

LH   When you publish or speak publicly, you can't get away from the fact that people are making notes, and not always of what you would like them to. It is unfortunate that he was not happy with the use of his name in the title, although I am sure he wasn't too seriously hurt by it. I used it to make it specific, it was from a certain event. You have to accept that people will interpret things in different ways, taking notice of some things and not of others – which is what will be happening in this situation today. I think again it is the distinction between a tenderness towards that which may be ignored and a questioning of authority. With the guidebooks, they seem different now from how they did at the time; humorous because not only is the place not there, but they are describing them in such a flowery, Soviet way that they seem laughable. Obviously that's not how they were meant. Over time, anything you put out into the public domain is seen differently. You can't get away from misinterpretation.

Audience *The issue of misinterpretation also seems to link to an ethic of care, as with all of these projects, saving the words, hunting out things which no longer exist, trying to care for them when they are precisely the thing we generally don't care for.*

LH If there are things we are supposed to take notice of, which turn out to be ridiculous or don't make sense, you may as well look at something else. You may as well categorize all the emotions in a shelf full of books as anything else. Why is it just the names that you categorize, not what's happening in the books?

JC *My interest is in the lecture piece. I could well envisage the private neurosis of noting down all these 'umms' and 'ahhs' and I thought of the work of social scientists and applied linguists who actually do that kind of thing with discourse markers, presenting a text as a piece of empirical research. How do we decide which bits of text are important or can we decide that? Does your work really examine how we make such a decision or are you saying that's what it does and actually, it does something else?*

LH I was presenting a lecture using the mechanics of the lecture theatre and representing the words in that space. I am not getting down to exactly what's happening with all those words, but you know, I'm only an artist.

SK *Thinking of Benjamin and* The Arcades Project, *the figures of the city for Benjamin are the flâneur, the gambler, the sandwichman, the detective and the prostitute. Woman in the city is a fleeting presence. A French term for prostitute is* péripatéticienne, *literally, a woman who walks around. What are you?*

LH I am a different thing at different times – the female figure in the city is an interesting one, as women haven't always had the same freedoms. Janet Wolff also points out that women in city-based narratives often end up as murder victims. Some of my work has looked at the detective and this may be similar to how I make my work, the collecting of clues and evidence. However, my way of navigating the city has changed over the years and now I am a typical 'Londoner' who tends to give the impression of ignoring what and who is around in public. When I am collecting in London, it's generally things I start noticing going about my everyday business. It could look like the way a detective might work; I am trying to find things in Tallinn and Riga which I am being told are there, but I can't really find them.

CA   *There is a real sense of melancholy for something that is lost in your work in Tallinn and Riga. You go into it as an outsider, as a western European tracing aspects that are forgotten and lost. When you ask people, do you remember where this building was, they don't know. There's a collective sense of denial about a past that they would choose to forget.*

LH   Yes, even though the loss of those aspects of the Soviet era was a positive change, there is still the sense of melancholy involved with a description of something that has disappeared without a trace. I have tried to make clear in the text I've used that I'm not nostalgic for something that I didn't experience. It's not my place to do that, but I feel that if something as big as this can disappear, be forgotten, then so can anything else. I was working with an artist in Tallinn who was in the Soviet army for a few years. He had a terrible time yet he still, because of his childhood memories, feels nostalgia for the era. With *Detour*, we were comparing our perception of the city as two foreign visitors, with the version that was in the two books that we were using, and they could both be imaginary. They are melancholic in that you get to these places and there is nothing there.

NA   *How did you find out about the initials in the back of the library books?*

LH   I spent some time in the library and when I was looking for notes in the margins I found this system of notation of readers in the back which the librarians explained to me they were very frustrated about. It's strange that you would have no idea whether you had read a book if you didn't initial it.

NA   *Do you work with a designer?*

LH   I design them myself or sometimes in collaboration with another artist. I see that process as an important part of making the work.

EC   *I am intrigued by the debate that happens in that margin space. I can't think of any other place where you could have a debate that spans decades. It plays with the time zones very effectively. Does this sense of passage of time operate in other ways in your work – I am thinking particularly about the guidebook texts?*

LH   There is something important about things being outdated as well as being just generally unreliable. Things become outdated the moment they're published. I am interested in W. G. Sebald's writing, the way he describes how unbelievable it is that something can just disappear, and that's how I feel when I read those descriptions.

Audience *You said those people – those whose names you collected from shop signs – were imposing themselves onto the city. This is similar to the people initialling the back of the books, putting their own stamp on something that isn't theirs. Do you want to find a place within something where your own personal place isn't obvious? If you read a book you might not take anything from it, you walk through a city and you may not get anything from it, but there is always a desire to impose on it nonetheless.*

LH A guidebook wouldn't have my own experiences in it, that's why it is not a true guide. When I first started listening to conversations and noting them down, it was partly an interest in public places and how words and language might exist in public places differently from private places. Cities can seem very impersonal, large and unfriendly, but at the same time there are moments when you see something personal. That's why I like making books, because they can be portable, something that you can put in your pocket. The intrusion of the personal into the public place of the city is important.

Audience *Is making your books is a way of doing that, like these names you are trying to leave a trace of yourself by making books that will then go into catalogues, that people will talk about? Then someone might see your name and see the book. Is that imposing a part of yourself in a public form, like a catalogue? Is that why you make books in editions?*

LH I like making them in editions so they can exist in different places and contexts. They don't have to be precious; they can be used to prop up a table. I like the idea that if something has a different meaning when you put it in a different context, then if you have a thousand things, then you have a thousand different possibilities.

Opposite:
Lucy Harrison
Guided Tour (Riga)
2005
Digital print
One from a series of 46, each 25.4 x 20.3 cm

*The Lenin Museum is now being used as an office building.
I knocked on the door but nobody answered,
despite a man being visible at a downstairs window.*

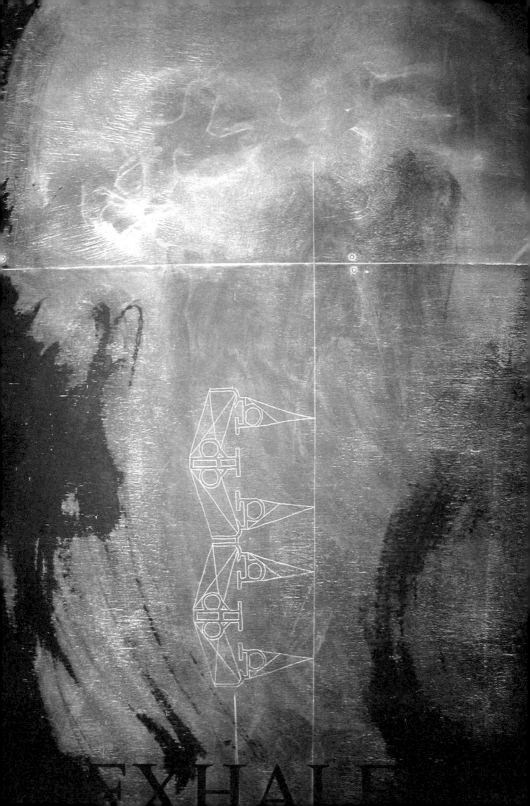

EXHALE

Brigid McLeer

Brigid McLeer's practice is generally image/text based and cross-disciplinary, moving between the practices of visual art, writing, architecture, performance and critical theory. Recent work has been shown and published in Britain, USA and Ireland. McLeer currently teaches in Diploma History and Theory at the Bartlett School of Architecture, London and on MA Fine Art at Goldsmiths College; and is a visiting lecturer on a number of arts courses in Britain. She was a lecturer in Performance Writing at Dartington College of Arts, Devon from 1995-2000. She trained in Fine Art at the University of Ulster, Belfast and the Slade School of Art, London.

In articulating a framework of reference for her lecture, McLeer described her current practice as located in the interplay between writing and drawing, at the point at which text and visual elements collide and issues of legibility become more active. McLeer positioned the concerns of the work as those of place, site, and process. In *Firsts of Placing* (1997) and *Deixis (absence of what qualifies this surface?)* (1998), the page itself or material substance is a site or space in which the work takes place. Inscription becomes an act performed or scored upon its surface; the page bleeds into and out of the work. In *Habitat* and *In Place of the Page*, the process-based aspects become cumulative, gathering a momentum through which numerous outcomes materialise, are reused, remade or reconfigured. McLeer explores how place itself is inscribed within us through our memories, and how meanings or cultural codes and expectations are inscribed onto us through the larger socio-cultural effects of language, history, and myth. In the work, inscription could be understood as the operations of writing, as well as of 'mark-making', as both a sign and a scar.

Contributors   *Sylvia Brandstetter, Sharon Kivland, Tom Newell, Julie Westerman*
Chair   *Emma Cocker*

EC   *As the lecture programme continues, the relationship between the talks develops. I'm sure there are many of you who will notice the parallels and the over-writing that happens as the speakers talk about their practices. It is intriguing how people have approached similar themes yet present a different outcome. I am interested in the ideas of texts as filters through which to re-examine existing information in your work.*

BMcL   The status of the work is always renegotiated. Text exists to do a particular job – but I might work with a text in such a way that it doesn't do that job. For instance, in my rewriting of the dictionary, the intention of the dictionary and the assumption of language – that language can be defined – is undone as it's made visual. Many elements in the work are filters. As activities occur, or collaborations happen, so there is a constant sense of uncertainty in the work.

EC   *Both in the talks and in knowledge acquisition, I have a struggle with points of illumination and points at which the over-writing muddies...*

BMcL   The process of making work is that process. I'm interested in bringing
       to the surface what underlies – not just the process of making art,
       but life in general in different ways – muddying, or ambivalence or
       mystery, as well as moments of acuity and sense.

Audience   *You did pick out some words though, and I'm interested in what led you to*
       choose those in particular, as in the drawings you'd made from the blackboards,
       where 'exhale' was clearly written.

BMcL   The process produces something, like a set of images. Then I work
       with the images, pushing their meaning into a more particular
       position. In that piece, photographs are taken during the day with
       a digital camera, then I edit from the material, extracting particular
       resonances that I feel are in that image. It's a process of finding –
       'meaning' is too broad a term for it – an instance of communication
       or an instance of something occurring in the work. Those words
       seemed to do something more to the image to bring out its qualities.
       In general, there are words that I find myself living with for a while.
       In earlier work, prepositions were important: 'here', 'there'. 'pre-',
       'post-', suffixes as well. Often a word will operate as a fulcrum to a
       project. Also words that are internally resonant like 'asunder' and 'as
       under'. There's an attention to the play of individual words. It changes
       in how I make a choice.

Audience   *When you were making the text plans from the e-mails, and then subsequently*
       making architectural plans, did you and the architect, Katie Lloyd Thomas,
       have any rules?

BMcL   I didn't have any rules other than unconscious ones that were
       formalized as the process went on. When I began, I could only work
       with the text from the e-mails; I couldn't introduce any new text.
       Neither of us have a procedure that would mean that anybody
       could make the work through his or her own application. One of
       the first things that I do with a text plan is change its scale, either by
       photocopying or by scanning the text into the computer; its scale is
       shifted so it becomes more structural, more visual. I knew I could not
       possibly illustrate the e-mails, which were complex, like short letters.
       The text plans aren't an attempt to visually describe the e-mail, but
       they are a visual transposition or treatment. Katie's process is more
       obvious and she doesn't work digitally. She did set herself some rules.
       She decided that she had to impose a scale for the drawing, to decide
       whether she was looking at a plan, section or elevation. She uses the
       texts in the drawing as clues or instructions. Other than that, her
       process of deciding what is there is as intuitive as mine. In the early
       stages, we would meet after she'd done six or seven of the text plans

and we'd decide how they fitted together. She might make a detail of a tiny section through a door in one plan, and a site plan in another. They were fragmentary but now we know so much more about the building, it's more difficult for her because there are bits missing and she wants the information to fill in that bit. It's a more intuitive process than some of the other generative procedural projects might be.

Audience *What is the final outcome? Did you have a plan of the building at the end?*

BMcL We're still doing it. It will be an architectural proposal, but not a completely drawn-up proposal. We could do that, but that would require more funding. With this project, as with others, there isn't one single final work. That's important to me because otherwise I carry these projects around for years. Because we're working collaboratively, it's also something that I can't decide by myself. In working with me, Katie's not working purely as an architect, so her drawings are not operating in a conventional architectural way.

EC *I am interested in the momentum of the work. You talked of it as originating from a hub. You spoke of not trying to 'execute' the work, and the double reading of that word I found particularly interesting in relation to the idea of momentum. How do you know when to stop? Is that the role of the collaborator?*

BMcL I have given up worrying about stopping. It's not such a big deal, you know. It's more about how you identify when there is a work that can exist in its own right as an object. That might mean not just an object, an image or a published text. It might mean an object as in a live installation. I find it much more difficult to think about starting than stopping. *In Place of the Page* and *Habitat* are overtly concerned with the difficulty of stopping, the difficulty of the object, of location. They're trying to activate that difficulty. Rather than just picture it or describe it, they're also trying to enact or activate it. They reflect on their own process and they produce themselves, like a Moebius strip. They produce the ability to reflect as well. In recent works, I am interested in setting out from the beginning to produce something that is insistently an object. It is a relief to be able to do that. The work is being executed overtly. It's a great word, 'execute', because of its connotations and I use it jokingly, because of the idea that you might kill something by bringing it into being.

JW *I was struck by the complexity of the process and your engagement; you talk about projects taking years to come to fruition. Is there a distance between that and how the viewer has access? The process is completely engaging, but the parts seem like the tip of an iceberg. As the viewer, I'm stuck with just this tip, and – I don't know whether it's lost in reality – I want the rest of the stuff to come through. The last work you showed was a contained, intense piece, which came across clearly whereas in others you only give 'markers' that are simplistic compared to the complexity of the process.*

BMcL *In Place Of the Page*, the collaborative project with the architect, began as a private process, an e-mail exchange between ten people. The series of steps that happen after are also essentially private processes. After a time, I decided that I wanted to make the project public, and that was through the website – *inplaceofthepage.co.uk* – There you can read all the emails, see all the completed text plans and the architectural drawings. Then we decided to do live showings, and the ways in which people accessed it changed. The intention was to address what you're talking about. How does the project in its different facets communicate itself to somebody else who knows nothing about it? We developed certain solutions in that instance but there could be others. Because I'm interested in process, in *In Place of the Page* I set up an exhibition where a process would be happening that someone could engage with. *Habitat* is slightly more complicated, each time it gets the chance to become public, it's reconfigured because it's made of different elements. I've shown it in presentations, some of it has been published; I've made pieces for the page from it. There are some video pieces that have been shown. It's been shown as a work in progress. But I haven't yet had a chance to really explore how it would work as a gallery piece and so it hasn't really been finalized as a set of 'objects'.

JW *Is there a difference between the pieces of work that are made with an end product and those made as a process? The alphabet pieces, for instance, seem very immediate for an audience to engage with, because one can imagine you in the process of doing it and there's an immediate pleasure in the final image. Your practice produces pieces, but the practice itself seems far more important than the product.*

BMcL There's a difference of intensity and of outcome. *Habitat* is a sprawling work about the laterality of the process of making. I'm doing what I'm doing, but I'm never doing what I'm doing on my own. Nobody is. What has been produced or said always inscribes anything that anybody tries to produce or to say subsequently. It's about the myth of whiteness, whiteness in terms of the blank page, the empty studio, the sublime void. That's where all these references to the Arctic and explorers come in. There is the myth that there is something that has never been done, a place that has never been charted, that the human spirit can wrest this from the void. So it's trying to produce a space that undermines that intensity. Whereas the writing out of the dictionary undermines something else in a different way, requiring an intense focus, an accretion of its status as an object because it's sucking in the extension of language into these drawings / writings...

JW   *All the information is there, isn't it?*

LH   It's all there. If you believe me, of course.

SK   *Alain Robbe-Grillet's novel* La Jalousie – *as you read out the description of the woman as you're writing it, the way you speak it as you're writing – is written in the present tense, as though it's in the act of happening. The closest analogy I find is the cricket commentary, 'a pigeon is flying overhead', 'a seagull has landed on the field' and so on. That's another kind of narration in the present, and a narration in the present is one without resolution, because there is as yet no punctuation. It hasn't entered history, a past tense. There's a certain tension in listening to it, because it's endless. In your bridge work, a phrase appears: 'without stress and tension'. I know it's a play on building methodology, but nonetheless: 'without stress and tension, there is collapse and fall'.*

LH   There's a video that I would have loved to have shown you – I decided not to because it's fifteen minutes long – it has that quality of tension through duration. There is an attention to the present and a tension in the present. The work is always attentive to what it is doing, now and across time. That's where it becomes – depending on your experience of it – either interesting or frustrating because there's a sense of never getting to the point. I'm interested that the work might produce – not exactly openness – a vibration. In order to experience the work you have to take part in it, as viewer or reader. On a simple level that may be like the laying of the acetate on the pages of the published piece. On a more complex level, it's as you describe with *La Jalousie*. That is the nature of that novel. Also I forgot to mention that 'la jalousie' means Venetian blinds, so obviously the drawing is picturing that. It's early stages; I'm only a quarter of the way through the book.

EC   *Can 'presentness' as a moment of narrative exist only if it's spoken? Does it make no sense if it's transcribed or written, because there then can be an oscillation between past and present in a way that there can't be with the spoken voice?*

BMcL You can activate the present of the reading through something that occurs in writing. The reader becomes the present. I don't want to fetishize the present either, but in order to negotiate it, you have to enter into it.

TN   *Some works seem to rely on a sense of mystery – is that intentional? One example, when the names of the books flashed up quickly, we weren't given enough time to read them.*

BMcL That was fast partly because there are a lot of them. But they were never properly attended to as books. I read a lot of them, but not all. I didn't read them fully; I didn't read them particularly well or reverently. That's why in that piece you see words saying 'poach', 'rob', 'pilfer', 'steal', drawing attention to the fact that I was mining them to use them for my own purposes. So I flick them up there so that you can see them, but you can't attend to them. Mystery is a good word for much that occurs in the work – I would probably call it 'ambiguity' – trying to articulate what doesn't add up. The dilemma for me as an artist is getting the balance right where something is communicated, so a viewer can engage with the work, while sustaining the sense of exploration, mystery, ambiguity or ambivalence. It's up to you to decide whether that's successful or not. I am interested in letting that through as a condition. Somebody once said to me that the work revelled in getting lost.

EC *The work reminds me of archaeological sites, with its buried information. This connects to the idea that you're given markers or clues but there's something deeper beneath the surface.*

BMcL Making work is a mysterious process. Creative endeavour is not something that proceeds from one point and moves logically to an endpoint. A friend describes it as 'reasoning backwards'; you move forward, you have something, then you have to read it back to yourself. It demands a certain kind of action – the work asks you to do things. Unless you enter into a relation with the work, you're always going to be executing it. I'm interested in discovery as an inevitability, but also as a method. As I am more aware of it, it becomes more tangible as a method. *In Place of the Page* is figured around methods of discovery as much as methods of translation. When Katie talks about the building, she's not exactly designing a building; rather she's deriving or divining a building. She's finding a building in the material and I'm finding visual images in the e-mails. That's not to suggest that there is no intention. It's not random.

SB *I'm interested in the dictionary piece, which is obviously process orientated. What other process – apart from writing out all the As, the Bs and Cs and so on, is there for you?*

BMcL There's a physical process. It's very hard to write out the dictionary! One of the reasons I engaged in this, is because I hardly write anymore. I type more than I write by hand. I was interested in what might happen if I forced myself into a situation where I have to write by hand. I have to go back to a bodily experience that is becoming increasingly remote to me. One of the processes is the pain in my hand; I have to stop. I can only do it in stages. It's going to take a long time because I have to stop for a couple of days for my wrist to recover. I'm not recording that process in any way; I'm not videoing it or recording it in sound so I can be lax about the environment. I might be listening to music. There are thought processes that occur. I also discover many new words while I'm doing it. The writing out of Robbe-Grillet's novel is different; because I'm reading out the text as I write, the process is more corralled and becomes meditative. I become aware of my body and its strain as a process. In the sound piece with the Robbe-Grillet novel, you'll hear me sighing, and the stress on my body appears in the voice.

EC   *In terms of the body and strain within the work, and in connection to inter-disciplinary practice, do you feel that as the artist you are a bridge between disciplines?*

BMcL An art-making process allows for a relief from function or programme, which is one of the things that makes it interesting to architects. In working with me, while Katie is concerned with the function of the building, she doesn't have to worry about it. The programmeless nature of art is its strength in that cross-disciplinary process. I am acting as a bridge because I tend to make the overtures. Once that connection has been made, it's obviously a two-way encounter. The people I work with bring material I wouldn't have thought of. Once the bridge has been built, you can go both ways.

EC   *The element of uncertainty and risk within the practice is interesting because while bridges are spaces of security, or energy or flow; they are also risky spaces.*

BMcL I am a bridge. My family calls me 'Bridge'. *(Audience laughter)* The town I come from, Drogheda, that's an Anglicization of the Irish name, meaning 'bridge over the ford'. It's a key feature of what happens in the work: engaging with discrete conditions, bringing them together in a way that constitutes an object but also creates a dialogue. Something is reconstituted through the dialogue. Bridges are fantastic structures. They're compelling as physical objects. They're easy to read architecturally. The thing that looks most like its architectural drawing is a bridge. Yet they're fantastically conceptual things. They're made from a charge. They exist because of physical charge, stress and tension, and they also carry load and charge.

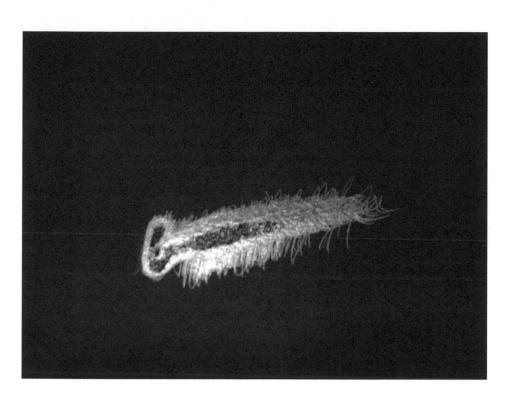

Brigid McLeer
Concise Chambers: 'b' (detail)
2005
From the 'Writing-Out' series
Pencil on paper
89 x 59 cm

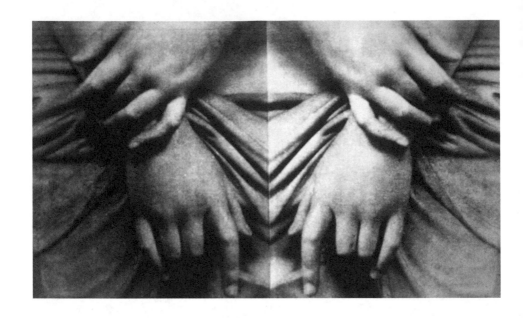

Vera Dieterich
The hand separates the hand from the hand
1997
Photographic screenprint
123 x 83 cm

08.03.05 Vera Dieterich and Caroline Rooney

Vera Dieterich and Caroline Rooney came together as a practitioner and as a theorist to explore shared interests in writing, in the notion of the text as a weave; and in philosophical and aesthetic questions pertaining to materiality and immateriality, the visible and the invisible. They recently collaborated on *Book Unbinding: The Ontological Stain* (London: Artwords Press 2005), in which they examined notions and operations of folding, cutting and binding as found in writing and art. Vera Dieterich lives and works in London, and lectures in Fine Art at Sheffield Hallam University. Her work is held in the permanent collection of the Staatsgalerie Stuttgart, Germany and she regularly exhibits in Europe. Caroline Rooney teaches at the University of Kent. She works in the areas of postcolonial literature and literary theory and is the author of *African Literature, Animism and Politics* (2000).

Referring to their collaborative research, to theorists and writers including Hélène Cixous, Jacques Derrida, Luce Irigary and Maurice Merleau-Ponty, and to recent visual work, the lecture embodied the notion of the text as a weave. Its fabric, at times rich and layered, was marked by the overlap of voices, by the merging of practices, and by the delicately woven articulation of ideas focusing upon the inter-relation between thinking and writing, sight and touch, distance and proximity. The lecture played out in fluid rhythmical waves, as textual choreography, as a spoken dialogue echoing the folded, mirrored and repeated qualities of the visual imagery. Intent on displacing the individual in the making of a third hybrid text, the lecture echoed a video work in which 'two hands inscribe simultaneously on one divided surface'. Endlessly caught up in a reciprocal action of doubling and mirroring, one hand at first writes whilst another traces the inscription. Dieterich and Rooney say of their collaboration: 'Thus two minds attempt to merge in thought: this is where our position arises.'

Contributors   *John Clark, Julie Westerman*
Chair   *Emma Cocker*

Audience   *How does working together operate?*
CR   It begins with Vera's art; we approach it from different angles, a bit like the two directions of the hands meeting at a text – as we saw in the video – and then we try to create a third work from that encounter.
VD   As the thinking process remains undefined, I turn towards theoretical reading to clarify my own inner thoughts. This is also where both of our interests merge, as such we are located within the text and its context. We begin at a state of defined openness. The theoretical text enables me to see my unknowingness articulated and then it is fed back into the practice, not in order to illustrate it but to get a glimpse of my thought, to get a glimpse at what can never be defined. It's seeking a reflection between the self and the other within the text or the image. I suppose my work is centred on an elliptical sense of

reading. It begins with the perceived, which seeks its text and finds
its image and seeks its text and so on. Caroline's thought process is
located within the text and the text expands the reading of the image
while visualizing the text's theoretical aspects. Hence our hands meet,
we approach each other through the image and we are joined by the
hand that writes the text.

CR   It's good for me to visualize things that I think or conceptualise – to
actually see them.

EC   *The video that you showed with the two hands worked well in relation to
the idea of collaboration. You talked about the blind pen and the hand that
follows without knowing. I thought that was interesting in terms of the
conversation in which you are both following and shifting responsibility. Does
your collaboration follow a line of conversation?*

CR   That's a very good point actually. Sometimes we are talking about the
same thing but we are not always in synch. There are those slippages
and unexpected forks in direction to which one returns.

EC   *In collaboration, does this allow for greater uncertainty?*

CR   It makes me think that some of the stuff that I'm working with is too
schematic and so the uncertainty begins to de-sediment it, undo the
given formalisations.

Audience   *The text you presented was very beautiful, elegant and interwoven. The images
stand as very beautiful images but finally I'm struck by how mute the images
seem compared with the complexity of the dialogue between you, especially the
images where wallpaper is overlaid with a tracery. It seems to be looking back,
never forward. The muteness seems to establish an opposition.*

VD   I don't see it as an opposition.

CR   I sometimes feel as if I'm talking too much when I have those images.
It's interesting, that regress you see, but I think it takes you to the
point where everything begins and so the silence starts to open up
language. Vera was talking about the potential or the pre-script: there
are these ghostly traces leading you back, back to a sense of where
you can begin...

Audience   *Or even a sense of returning to absolute stillness or the point of turning,
neither forwards nor backwards, what is held in this absolute moment of
stillness of the turning world.*

CR   It's interesting that you should say that because that is what comes out
of our reading of T. S. Eliot's *Four Quartets*. Vera was saying the other
day that certain phrases that Eliot uses resonate with what we have
been talking about today. Eliot writes: 'In my beginning is my end'
and 'At the still point of the turning world'.

VD   It is its essence, I think. The muteness allows projection: my projection and the projection of the audience. And so I would like to refer to the part of Eliot's text that states: 'In order to arrive at what you are not you must go through the way in which you are not. And what you do not know is the only thing you know. And what you own is what you do not own. And where you are is where you are not.' [1] And in this sense the practice needs to shift within the realm of located-dislocation.

JW *The video that you started with seems about your collaboration, while other works are about Vera's work and the dialogue with Vera. The video seems to hold the potential for forward movement, because it's live in the act of making whereas these others are different. Would you comment on the possibility of a new dialogue?*

VD We have many new ideas so it is just the beginning. It has unleashed many possibilities.

JW *The work before the collaboration holds itself in an internal dialogue and maybe the collaboration has the possibility of opening a new external dialogue, from which I felt excluded in the earlier work.*

VD Do you think it is only my dialogue? Can't you project your own dialogue?

JW *I can but it is at a distance. The endless veils seem intended to keep one distanced.*

EC *Towards the end you were talking about scribbling and overwriting. I am interested in this as it is manifested in some of the rigorous texts to which you were returning. In coming to the point of zero and starting again, how do you understand the act of scribbling in terms of your practices?*

VD My entire practice is a scribble. It is finding a form but denying it, ending up with a form but rejecting it. It is a continuous process of erasure. The mark is linked to a confident hesitation that tends towards a denied definition. The text/image remains cryptic in its reading since the work is not about comprehension instead it locates the escape, the escaped text.

EC *Is it Derrida who writes about writing under erasure, writing that is inaccurate but is necessary to say in order to create a space or a gap? You talk about an interlude or a pause — what do you hope takes place in that space?*

VD I suppose a pause, an undefined gap that leads beyond the visual field. One seeks this muteness, this silence, which, as Edmond Jabès says, is 'sensitized by words'. And Jean-Luc Nancy speaks of a silence that comes neither before nor after speech but is rather a vibration between meanings. In an ideal sense the work becomes the 'vibration'.

CR For me too, it becomes a philosopheme of art. I like the phrase that we were revolving earlier, 'the other side of writing'. I was thinking there are two sides of writing. One side would be the tracing of it; the other side, the gap or *écart* of the trace, would be a feeling that is not yet writing...

EC   *... or reading. That's like the metaphor of the two pens meeting, like trying to listen, but at times it is too fast to follow and at other times it lags behind, unable to keep up with the pace – like listening in this context, having to catch up while being distracted.*

CR   The audience is one of the hands.

Audience   *Listening to your presentation, your voices, I was transported. The words completely lost their meaning. I forgot to listen altogether and it was a wonderful experience. What you said, all the texts you quoted, meant nothing to me, but the words back and forth were like a lullaby.*

EC   *Poetry has the capacity to puncture language. It loses the anchor of meaning.*

CR   I have been working with poetry because its rhythmic nature is a form of stuttering. There's the suspense of an unspecified 'all' that you can't say, also an 'all that you can't say'. Then when you start to say it, you have to stutter because you use a spatio-temporal medium. And in the art of the fold there may be a visual equivalent of this poetic stuttering.

EC   *I like this idea of putting yourself in this position of sediment, layers of knowledge. At a recent conference in Bristol, Mark Palmer was talking about how robots learn, putting forward that the more complex the robot's programming, the greater its tendency to stutter. You come to the point of not being able to talk, which has made me think of forgetting. How important is forgetting in getting past that stutter?*

CR   I love the idea of the robot stuttering!

EC   *It is because of your reference to Eve, the desire for knowledge and the subsequent desire for the reversal of knowledge, which I feel all the time in my relation to art and ideas. At times, I would like a forgetting to occur, so that I might encounter things afresh.*

JC   *I'm interested in your use of Derrida, who suggests writing as a mode of communication, an all-encompassing model of transcription. Does that affect your work?*

CR   I have been trying to question that because I work a lot with Derrida, and part of the de-sedimenting is part of different ways of deconstructing. One of the things that has somewhat bothered me in my encounter with Derrida is this enigmatic aphorism of his, which many have tried to interpret, about there being nothing outside of the text. So, one of the things which delighted me when I first saw the video which we have seen today was that you can actually see that what is outside of the text is the movement of writing, and that is where I would put speech, speech as animation. In following the movement of hands writing we were not able to see the formed text; equally, the formed text would imply this movement even if it were not visible as such.

Audience   *I am interested in the distinction you made between handwriting and using a machine/computer. As I understand Cixous, this is the writing from the body she describes. I understand this as coming from an unconscious or pre-symbolic source, so I wonder if it necessarily needs to be handwriting or could using a computer be a contemporary mode of writing, replacing handwriting, effectively doing the same thing?*

CR   I think that precisely what Derrida would be implying when he talks about this new logic is that the unconscious might be already a sort of machine, although I myself am not sure about this.

Audience   *To some degree, writing with the hand is being replaced and that it is in the same mode of writing as Cixous describes it. It is just that the method is replaced.*

VD   Cixous refers to the entire body and the body in relation to the hand that inscribes, so there is a connection between the touch of the hand and the paper. With the computer, there is another – the keyboard – between the body and page.

CR   When you type, you are obliged to type key by key even if you are going very fast, whereas with a piano keyboard you can make chords. I wonder if this has something to do with it.

EC   *Do you think then that the act of typing it puts writing into performing with a linear trajectory?*

CR   I am still wondering about it, but I think so. I think it is a question of rhythm, of whether you submit to the machinic rhythm – plonk, plonk, plonk – or whether the instruments of writing are subordinate to the rhythm of writing.

EC   *You talk about the book-less script and the script-less book – how does this connect to the body, the fold and the fabric with a relation to formlessness?*

CR   In the same way that when something is always in movement, it resists any form; that is what I was trying to address.

EC   *In Cixous' text the language concerns waves and outbursts and spillage and excess, as though this is the language with which to talk about desire and experience and feelings rather than in a linear way.*

CR   With the wave, I am also interested in the movement of inversion, like a figure-of-eight that moves back and forth from those fluid elements. There is an emerging from containment that can, at a certain point, recoil, turn round upon itself and dissolve back into envelopment.

EC   *At a recent conference at Sheffield University on architecture and the body,*

Doina Petrescu, in a paper titled 'Bodies, Folds and Strange Minds', spoke
of the connection between folds and hysteria, which is spoken of in Surrealism
as a fold of expression. She argued that the fabric and the fold represent the
nineteenth-century hysteric. She was also talking about Bernini. The images
that you showed reminded me of that.

CR I hadn't thought of that. What you are saying is really suggestive.
Yes, there is a veiled femininity and perhaps also elements of fetishism.
Thinking about it psychoanalytically what comes to mind is Lacan's
teacher, Clérambault, who took many photographs of folded
costumes, and so there has been a question if he was fetishizing the
fold. There is an interesting essay by Joan Copjec, who suggests that
he was interested in the fold's use value as a protest against capitalist
commodity fetishism. He was interested in the use value of the
clothing. I have always wanted to think of a category beyond use
value, the value of practice or a making by hand which takes on a
practice value.

EC *Is there a connection between the fold and curiosity, the unseen and invisible,*
particularly in the erotic, sensual quality of the photographs?

VD Of course I would like to seduce the viewer and lead them into their
own folds of perception.

CR There is fluidity in the visual material and the way the text was spoken.

Audience *Does the work remain unfulfilled?*

VD Absolutely. That is its essence. The work's sense of 'vibration' is
continuously disrupted.

Audience *Yet if one returns to some images, there is promise of fulfilment – the tips of*
the pens meet in the act of foreplay.

VD But it is the line in-between that you see, it is meeting but it is not
meeting so it still has the potential of a gap. It refers back to this
sense of located dislocation, the pens continuously slide ahead or
behind of each other, while aiming to find the groove of the other.
Its dislocation becomes its pleasure, the dance or chase one meets in
order to catch one's breath.

CR That was a funny part of our collaboration, because I wanted to
emphasise the contact and Vera kept talking about the divide and
the gap, so we were looking at different things, the word 'contact'
and the word 'divide'. Of course, the point of contact is also the
point of division.

Audience *One hand is allowed to have dominance over the other as time goes on.*

EC *How do you feel about the metaphors of fabric and the fabric of writing – as in*
frays and rips or punctures?

VD I suppose the practice attaches itself to the frays – the rupture. A place where the trace has been dislocated while attaching itself to the weave of form / language.

EC *The seam – or tear – is the point where ideas overlap, the point where people come together through dialogue, conversation or collaboration.*

CR It's like that, a forking of lines or a rip, which is something I really like, such as the ripping of a piece of paper. It creates an impromptu dynamic, one of pull and counter-pull.

EC *The project you collaborated on is a book. How does that operate in terms of formlessness, because the book is a finite form, isn't it? Would you consider other presentation methods that are less bordered?*

VD Well this is one, today.

CR We would have to think about that. Also, in our book we tried to enact a book that is in the process of unbinding, unravelling or ruining itself as it went along.

Audience *There was an incredible relation between the words and the images you showed, both were crafted, fragile and stripped down. What is the balance between them?*

VD It is peculiar because the words are not that much different from the images. I almost create the same with the words as I do with the images. But the words are different because I quote from other people. In a way, through this collaboration, I seem to have found the image through language. I am continuously searching for a reflection of my internal image in the image of an object or the image of a text.

Audience *Was that really your internal landscape?*

VD It is hidden within the fold and the illegible.

EC *Would you speak about play and spending time with the work? For me, the lecture and the quality of the image suggested that time is spent in the processes of making and writing that connects to playfulness?*

CR I think there is a nice sense of a 'let be' or seeing what is possible.

EC *There seem to be many references to searching and taking pleasure in getting lost.*

CR There is surprise when that happens. Also when one unexpectedly stumbles across someone who has written something that goes well with what one does.

EC *Is that what conversation is, trying to find people, to find that thread, that point of connection?*

VD Absolutely.

CR Yes.

JW *I would like you to explore the notion of disrupting the work, which comes into the play of the work. Your work is so exquisite and it seems to hold one at a rarefied moment. Do you never want to scribble on it?*

VD   No.

JW   *Not even to open up the idea? Do you never want to trample it on the floor?*

VD   No.

CR   Sometimes I would like to write something next to Vera's work.

JW   *Don't you want to scream next to it?*

CR   Or laugh because that seems so inappropriate. I think it is better when such reactions are next to the work rather than in it.

VD   The tension is amplified by its muteness, which also locates the silent scream. As Caroline mentioned the inappropriate, the dissonance next to the work can also re-emphasize this intrinsic silence. Each aspect emphasizes the other.

CR   But I also feel uncertain about it.

VD   No, it really works. There is a peculiar awkwardness about the purity of a thought. It is silence. The unthinkable thought.

Audience   *Do you really want or strive for that silence?*

VD   I strive for silence.

EC   *Is that a desire for the interlude, the pause or the suspended moment? Pockets of silence?*

VD   Shutting it down, a non-space, because graffiti is around me all the time.

1   T. S. Eliot, *The Four Quartets*, London: Faber & Faber 1979.

Opposite:
Vera Dieterich
Untitled
2005
Photographic screenprint
123 x 83 cm

Symposium

Site-Writing

Jane Rendell

With a background in architectural design, followed by research in architectural history, and then a period teaching public art and writing art criticism, my work has focused on interdisciplinary meeting points – feminist theory and architectural history, conceptual art practice and architectural design, art criticism and autobiographical writing.[1]

Recently my writing has explored the position of the author, not only in relation to theoretical ideas, art objects and architectural spaces but also to the site of writing itself. This interest has evolved into a number of site-writings that investigate the limits of criticism, that ask what it is possible for a critic to say about an artist, a work, the site of a work and the critic herself and for the writing to still 'count' as criticism. This paper outlines some conceptual concerns that frame this project before discussing a site-writing.

***

In postmodern feminism new ways of knowing and being have been discussed in spatial terms, using words such as 'mapping', 'locating', 'situating', 'positioning', and 'boundaries'. Employed as critical tools, spatial metaphors constitute powerful political devices for examining the relation between identity and place. Where I am makes a difference to who I can be and what I can know. For example, Donna Haraway's 'situated knowledges', Jane Flax's 'standpoint theory' and Elsbeth Probyn's notion of 'locality', all use 'position' to negotiate such on-going theoretical disputes as the essentialism/constructionism debate.[2] In bell hook's passionate claim for the margin to be understood and occupied as a place of radical difference, the exploration of race, class and gender identities is explicitly spatialized.[3] And in Rosi Braidotti's figure of the 'nomadic subject', a spatial state of movement describes an epistemological condition, a kind of knowingness (or unknowingness) that refuses fixity.[4] I am interested in how art criticism can engage with these concerns and investigate the spatial and often changing positions between works, the sites they are located in and the standpoints we occupy as critics materially, conceptually and ideologically.

When Hal Foster discusses the need to rethink critical distance, he points to the different distances produced by the optical and the tactile, but warns of the dangers of both dis-identification and over-identification with the object of study.[5] Foster rejects those who lament the end of 'true criticality' as well as those who see critical distance as 'instrumental mastery in disguise'. But despite advocating the need to think through questions of critical distance, Foster ends his reflection still proposing that the critic's role is to judge and make decisions without discussing the particularities of these modes of operation.[6]

Howard Caygill presents us with a different point of view, one that discerns between discriminations and judgements. For Caygill, in immanent critique the criteria for making judgements are discovered or invented through the course of criticism.[7] Caygill argues that there is no position outside the work from which the critic may make a judgement, rather a critic may make a discriminate judgement by adopting a position at a moment of externality where the work 'exceeds itself' and 'abuts on experience'. Strategic critique may use such moments in order to locate the work, and although Caygill does not acknowledge them as such, such procedures are intrinsically spatial:

> Strategic critique moves between the work and its own externality situating the work in the context of experience, and being in its turn situated by it.[8]

In art criticism few critics have taken a close interest in the experience of an encounter with a work. Mieke Bal is an exception. As Norman Bryson points out, Bal's work is rhetorical; she considers visual art through narrative and structures her own narratives through processes of focalization.[9] Yet despite Bal's ability to 'write' the encounter with a work of art, writing does not engage with the spaces of such encounters. When Nicholas Bourriaud calls for a 'relational aesthetics', he tends to locate the relational in the open-ended condition found in works by certain artists rather than in the spatial aspects of critical negotiation.[10] From the close-up to the glance, from the caress to the accidental brush, my interest in the site of encounter with art investigates the spatial qualities of relations.

To move beyond notions of judgement and discrimination in criticism to consider questions of relation and encounter, involves objective and subjective modes of enquiry as well as the taking of distant and intimate positions. Italo Calvino has explicitly explored the relation the writer has to his/her writing in terms of different subject identities or 'I's.[11] And Roland Barthes has described his choice of authorial voice in terms of four regimes: including an 'I', the pronoun of the self, a 'he', the pronoun of distance and a 'you', a pronoun which can be used in a self-accusatory fashion or to separate the position of the writer from the subject.[12] Feminists in cultural, literary and post-colonial criticism, such as Hélène Cixous and Gloria Anzaldua, have woven the autobiographical into the critical in their texts, combining poetic writing with theoretical analysis to articulate hybrid voices.[13] Yet fewer writers have acknowledged the position of the writing subject, the place of the personal and the role of the autobiographical in art criticism.

From those who theorise to those who tell stories, from those who list items to those who describe personal memories, from dictionary definitions to records of informal conversations, from artists' statements to critics' observations, from the walk through the gallery to an alternative space from which to imagine a work, my interest is the multiplicity of voice and the variation of stand-point. Such an approach can draw upon the remembered, the dreamed and the imagined, as well as observations of the 'real', and challenges criticism as a form of knowledge with a singular and static point of view located in the here and now.

What happens when discussions concerning site-specificity extend to involve art criticism, and the spatial qualities of the writing become as important in conveying meaning as the content of the criticism?[14] My suggestion is that this kind of criticism has concerns that go beyond writing 'about' art. In operating as a mode of practice in its own right, this critical writing questions the terms of reference that relate the critic to the art work positioned 'under' critique. This writing is spatial, it is an active writing that constructs as well as traces the sites between critic and writer, artist and art work, viewer and reader.

***

In 2001 when Jules Wright asked me to write about *Spring*, a work by Elina Brotherus she had commissioned for the Wapping Project in London, I found myself turning to three short texts I had written concerning three sites – two remembered, one dreamed. *Spring* was composed of two installations: a video triptych, *Rain, The Oak Forest and Flood*, in the boiler house and a back-lit image *Untitled*, showing a pale grey Icelandic sky over lava covered in moss, reflected in the water tank on the roof. A work that anticipates spring, the work opened in Wapping just after the autumn equinox in the northern hemisphere. Brotherus' interest in longing and my own in nostalgia provided me with three positions from which to consider her work in relation to themes of longing, nostalgia, anticipation and yearning.

Moss Green

It's a beautiful house – a one-storey building, with a square plan –
born at the birth of modernism in the aftermath of the First World
War. It embodies the values of early English modernism, of the arts and
crafts movement: 'truth to materials' and honest craftsmanship. From
the road it looks a little unloved, in need of some care and attention.
Up close it is clearly derelict, almost in ruins. We enter a room with
windows at each end. Curtains are falling away from the runners. The
fabric has been soaked overnight and is drying in the spring afternoon
sunshine. On the window sill and spilling over onto the floor are piles
of old magazines. The pages are stuck together and disintegrate if
you pull them apart. There are some photographs of buildings. One
is particularly damp, the corners are soft, the surface is wrinkled. It
shows a tower block, just completed, empty and pristine, a moss green
utopia, the modernist dream dispersing as it soaks up spring rain.

Moss Green, photograph by Jane Rendell, 2001

White Linen

I dreamt of the house last night. My mother's house in Cwmgors,
South Wales, a place where it always rained in the holidays, that as a
girl I resented, but now as it is being taken from me, I already begin
to miss. I was in the dining room; the rest of the house was empty
except this one room. The furniture was far too big and covered in
linen. The air was thick and still, silent. With the curtains drawn, it was
very dark, but the linen glowed white. I went towards the mantelpiece
to take a look at myself in the mirror, and I saw for the first time in
the reflection, that the room was full of plants; so alive I could smell
moisture still on their leaves.

White Linen, photograph by Jane Rendell, 2004

Bittersweet

In Palafrugell, a small town north of Barcelona on the Costa Brava is a derelict cork factory with a clock tower in front. The clock tower is a handsome structure, elegant and robust, but the clock on top has stopped. The floor is covered in dust and pieces of furniture, lampstands, chairs and old printing machinery. There are words everywhere scattered all over the floor: burnt orange, turquoise, black and white, bittersweet. We stay in the factory a long time. We don't speak, just walk and look. Later, once we've left the building, he brings something to show me. It is a white sign with carefully painted black letters: 'Bittersweet'. I reach into my bag and pull out a clear square section rod; along one side of it letters printed onto cardboard are embedded in the perspex. From the top it is out of focus, but from the side, you can read it: 'Bittersweet'.

Bittersweet, photograph by David Cross, 2001

'Moss Green' describes a derelict house in the green belt where in early March we found photographs of a brave new world of modernist high-rise housing. Just after the autumn equinox, just after her death, I dreamt of the home of my Welsh great aunt. 'White Linen' recalls this dream, while 'Bittersweet' remembers a spring visit to an abandoned cork factory in Catalunya where we found the names of colours scattered over the floor.

Jane Rendell, *Les mots and les choses*,
in 'Material Intelligence', Entwistle Gallery, London, 2002
Photographed by the Entwistle Gallery

For an expedition to Seoul, as 'what is the colour of memory?' (April 2002), each text was translated into Korean and accompanied by its 'object': an album of photographs found at Moss Green, a white linen cloth, and the word 'bittersweet' found in the factory. The texts were translated back into written English from the Korean audio recordings for their journey to Los Angeles as 'the voice one cannot control' (November 2002). In moving, the words were translated from English to Korean and back again, from writing to speaking and back again. For 'Concrete Feedback' at SYARC, curated by artist Brandon La Belle, the three pairs of texts were placed along a corridor with three columns, each one either side of a column. Three audio installations positioned the Korean voice at the point were the texts could no longer be read together.

When the work moved again, this time to the Entwistle Gallery in London as *Les mots et les choses* for 'Material Intelligence' in 2002, three objects were re-inserted, sited in the slippage in language produced through translation and displacement. In *Les mots and les choses* (1966), translated into English as *The Order of Things*, Michel Foucault explores the ordering of relations between different cultural elements, for example, those that are real, those that represent, those that resemble, those that can be imagined.[15] Between words and things, between writing and speaking, between one place and another, this site-writing is a two-way inscription, real and imagined, dreamed and remembered, of sites written and writings sited.

1   See for example Jane Rendell, *The Pursuit of Pleasure: Gender, Space and Architecture in Regency London*, London: Athlone Press 2002; Iain Borden, Jane Rendell, Joe Kerr with Alicia Pivaro (eds), *The Unknown City: Contesting Architecture and Social Space*, Cambridge, Mass: The MIT Press 2001; Iain Borden and Jane Rendell (eds), *InterSections: Architectural History and Critical Theory*, London: Routledge 2000; Jane Rendell, Barbara Penner, Iain Borden (eds), *Gender, Space, Architecture: an Interdisciplinary Introduction*, London: Routledge 1999; Jane Rendell (ed.), *A Place Between*, special issue of *The Public Art Journal*, no.2, (October 1999).

2   See Jane Flax, *Thinking Fragments: Psychoanalysis, Feminism and Postmodernism in the Contemporary West*, Berkeley, Los Angeles: University of California Press 1991: 232; Donna Haraway, 'Situated Knowledges: the Science Question in Feminism and the Privilege of Partial Knowledge', *Feminist Studies*, vol.14, no.3, (Fall 1988), pp.575-603, especially, pp.583-8 and Elspeth Probyn, 'Travels in the Postmodern: Making Sense of the Local' in Linda Nicholson (ed.), *Feminism/Postmodernism*. London: Routledge 1990, pp.176-89, p.178.

3   See bell hooks, *Yearnings: Race, Gender, and Cultural Politics*, London: Turnaround Press 1989.

4   See Rosi Braidotti, *Nomadic Subjects*, New York: Columbia University Press 1994.

5   Hal Foster, *The Return of the Real: The Avant-Garde at the End of the Century*, Cambridge, Mass: The MIT Press 2001, pp.223-4.

6   Ibid., pp.225-6.

7   Howard Caygill, *Walter Benjamin: The Colour of Experience*, London: Routledge 1998, p.34 & p.79.

8   Ibid., p.64.

9   Norman Bryson, 'Introduction: Art and Intersubjectivity', Mieke Bal, *Looking in: The Art of Viewing*, Amsterdam: G+B International 2001, pp.1-39, p.12.

10 Nicholas Bourriaud, *Relational Aesthetics*. (trans. Simon Pleasance & Fronza Woods), Dijon: Les Presses du Réel 2002.

11 See Italo Calvino, *Literature Machine*. London: Vintage 1997, p.15.

12 See Roland Barthes, *The Grain of the Voice: Interviews 1962-80*. (trans. Linda Coverdale), Berkeley & Los Angeles: University of California Press 1991, pp.215-6

13 See Gloria Anzaldua, *Borderlands/La Frontera: the New Mestiza*. San Francisco: Lute Books 1999 and Hélène Cixous, 'Sorties', (trans. Betsy Wing) from Susan Sellers (ed.), *The Hélène Cixous Reader*. London: Routledge 1994.

14 On art and site-specificity see for example, Alex Coles (ed.), *Site Specificity: The Ethnographic Turn*. London: Black Dog Publishing 2000; Nick Kaye, *Site-Specific Art: Performance, Place And Documentation*, London: Routledge 2000; Miwon Kwon, *One Place After Another: Site Specific Art and Locational Identity*, Cambridge, Mass: The MIT Press 2002.

15 Michel Foucault, *The Order of Things: An Archaeology of the Human Sciences*, London: Routledge 1992, originally *Les Mots et Les Choses* Paris: Editions Gallimard 1966. This translation was first published in Great Britain in 1970 by Tavistock Publications Limited.

Jane Rendell is Reader in Architecture and Art and Director of Architectural Research at the Bartlett, UCL. An architectural designer and historian, art critic and writer, she is author of *The Pursuit of Pleasure*, (Athlone Press, 2001), editor of 'A Place Between', Public Art Journal, (October 1999) and co-editor of *Strangely Familiar*, (Routledge, 1995), *Gender Space Architecture*, (Routledge, 1999), *Intersections*, (Routledge, 2000) and *The Unknown City*, (MIT Press, 2000). She is currently completing a new book *From Art to Architecture* and working on a project of site-specific writings.

Implicasphere

Sally O'Reilly, with Cathy Haynes

The word 'implicasphere' is derived from Douglas R. Hofstadter's texts on artificial intelligence in which he explores the possibility of building machines that emulate the human brain. *Implicasphere* – a contraction of 'implication' and 'sphere' – refers to the associative capacities of human thought: the subjective connections made between concepts and images that are as much down to unconscious processes as empirical knowledge. The brain is structured by memories, emotions, associations, ideologies and other process-driven phenomena, and our implicaspheres represent a complex of nodes isolated from an historical accumulation of millions of brains. Of course, the activities executed by the human brain far exceed and arguably differ radically from those of the computer, but Hofstadter's aim is to examine the more useful capacities of consciousness beyond those of mere computation and transfer them to binary systems. His implicaspheres, then, would enable a computer to make leaps through logic and create shortcuts of imagination that would break the spell of a linear and exhaustive working out of things.

Our project *Implicasphere* perversely adapts Hofstadter's term for our own purposes. This gesture of 'lifting' is central to our project. With each issue we pick a theme that has both literal and metaphorical connotations – which so far have been string, mice, folly and roosters – and hold it up as a prism through which isolated fragments of material gleam, like milk-bottle tops to a magpie. Where Hofstadter aims to unleash a potentially infinite process of association through information technology, we confine ourselves to a single printed broadsheet. Unlike the compilation of an encyclopaedia or compendium, we are less concerned with order and 'original' context. Our editing process overrides linear concentrations of data, like a warm water bath lifting the labels off jam jars. Content for each issue is gleaned from second-hand bookshop, library and internet research as well as conversations with friends, acquaintances and total strangers. Our working process, then, is neither systematic, methodical nor linear; it is more an unfolding, studded with moments of serendipity and coincidence.

The *Implicasphere* project overwhelms hierarchies of typology by privileging thematic content over systematic categorization, disciplines or genres. The string issue, for instance, brought together, among other things, an excerpt from Patrick Hamilton's novel *Hangover Square*, in which the anti-hero weaves a web of twine around the living room of

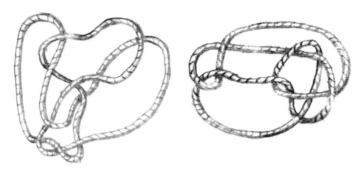

Two knots, adapted from Andrzej Solecki,
'Simple Crossing Projections of a Polygon'

his murdered victim, a comparison of two knots that were thought to be the same knot for seventy five years but were recently confirmed as different, and an ancient Lithuanian cure for a stammer that involves a piece of string knotted twenty seven times. The partial nature of these snippets is intended to provoke further associations for the reader. The extracts are also a way of teasing out subtexts that straddle disciplines, a way of slicing a pie in a different way. Within each cloud of association distinct links arise – a scientific, aesthetic or ontological development over centuries, perhaps. For instance, in 'Folly' an image from 1744, *The Pluralist (see opposite)* chimed wonderfully with Lewis Carroll's paradox of the perfect map, a map which was perfected and enlarged until it reached the scale of one mile to one mile; it's as if the Pluralist were navigating such a map on its way to 1:1 perfection. Links proliferate from issue to issue, which is always gratifying, and a single extract might find a home in more than one issue – as with *The Young Ones* scene when Rik Mayall finds a tampon in the woman's handbag – incorporating both string and mice.

Our model of a micro-universe is radiating, fragmentary and potentially infinite. So why have we chosen the medium of a single printed broadsheet? We are interested in incompletion and avoiding the linear structure of narrative. Each issue contains a short editorial essay, and is organised according to our own subjective 'implicaspheres'. But we aim never to exhaust a line of enquiry; threads are always left hanging for the reader to pick up. The placement of a text next to a certain image has, of course, an influence on the way that both are understood; each element has a viral potentiality, infecting the whole or, to put it another way, proximity inscribes meaning from one element to another, a significance that falls like a shadow.

Anon, *The Pluralist,*
1744, (courtesy of The British Museum)

Similarly, on another scale of consideration, the theme itself can be
seen to infect a whole library, a tranch of knowledge or raft of cultural
production. *Implicasphere* is an architecture made up of microsystems
embedded within macrosystems. A text of excerpts is itself an excerpt
of a potential but unimaginable whole, the familiar newspaper
broadsheet offering a structure of ordered columns to be unravelled.
Our influences include Victorian amateur lady botanists who collected
specimens without regard to taxonomy; almanacs that once combined
anecdotes, folklore, astrology and scientific data to predict the
agricultural year; 'Saturday Books' that sought to entertain families
with almost random selections of stories, facts and images to marvel
at; Georges Bataille's critical dictionaries in his Surrealist journal,
Documents; and the lists, journals and interviews of the Mass
Observation group, which attempted a cumulative portrayal of a
war-torn society. These various influences might be regarded as forms
of 'anti-totalising' texts that operate as constellations of fragments, in
the sense developed by Theodor Adorno and Walter Benjamin.
Implicasphere's material form – its status as 'imprint'– ironically fails to
contain its ephemeral content, its body built of fragments wrested
from context. Such failure exposes the instability of form at large,
embracing failure as generative and creative. *Implicasphere*, above all,
reflects the fleeting, chimeric nature of knowledge and understanding.

Sally O'Reilly is a critic and writer. She contributes regularly to Art Monthly, Modern
Painters, Frieze, Contemporary and Time Out magazines, has written numerous catalogue
essays and is co-editor of *Implicasphere* .

THIS PAGE IS INTENTIONALLY BLANK

Blank Page

Pavel Büchler

I would like to warn you that, unlike the previous speakers, I am not going to give a paper; this is going to be a presentation. There is a difference, not least a semantic one. These days we artists give papers; I remember a time when we used to use paper to make drawings. We presented those drawings in galleries. Now, in conferences, we confer our papers onto our audiences. To give a paper implies presentation, like giving a present. We present somebody with something which we believe that person or those people would like to have – a drawing or a text, perhaps. But what do you give to people, yourselves, who have just been presented so generously with so much?

To make a presentation means to make something present. We make presentations to call up something, bring it into the present, manifest its existence. Or at least, by the combined powers of imagination and photography, we conjure up a phantom presence: a projection on a screen. There was a time before PowerPoint presentations when we used to have slides, when pictures on the screen did not silently cut one to the next but every time you pressed the forward button there was a short gap, like a word space, and the reassuring mechanical noise of the moving parts of the slide projector to let you know that the machine was working as intended and the show would shortly resume.

All I am going to give you, for the present, is a blank page. Well, not even that. Here *(opposite)* is picture of a photocopy of the back page of the Association of University Teachers' National Executive ballot papers of 2001. The text, printed prominently in the middle, claims that 'this page is intentionally blank'. Something is not quite right about this. Obviously the page is not blank, let's face it. On the other hand, it is intended to be perceived as blank, surely.

In every act of writing, written communication, anything on a piece of paper (which is not what I'm giving today, but what I'm trying to make present), intentions seem to be mixed from the start. I want to present to you a blank page, but can't leave it just as I was left with it in the trade union booklet, intentionally blank. The true intention of the author of the page, the AUT returning officer, is not to give me any blank pages in my ballot papers, no bare, self-evident blankness. He makes this absolutely clear; there can be no confusion. Just imagine the panic that the paid-up trade union members like myself would feel if we received blank pages. The author anticipates my intention, that of the reader, who wants to get something from the page for his £9.20

not forms and colors

after Joseph Kosuth after Douglas Huebler after Lawrence Weiner ... *Artforum*, Vol. 36, No.3, 1997, p. 16

a month union fees. Now, what can I get from a blank page? Nothing, presumably. Can I get any more from one that offers me a proposition that is true only if it is false? The third intention is the intention of the page itself. It wants to be blank. That's what the text articulates, against the author's intentions, and what I must recover, as the author intended, so that from the page, overruled by the tautology of the sentence, I get something that I may only get from a blank page that speaks for itself. The words 'this page is intentionally blank' complement and contradict what I see as much as what I read. Paradoxically, the page would be blank only if it was not meant to be so. What it says is not what it wants to say and what it shows is not what it wants to show.

Ever since about 1750 we have been told that works of art are particularly good at having their own intention, a quality that makes the work simultaneously invite and resist interpretation by permitting improbable readings despite of what is written or shown, seen or read. The intention of the work is what the author and the reader have to negotiate to make present what is already 'there'— and at the same time respect that what is there is never fully uncoverable.

What is there when there seems to be nothing? Not forms or colours, to be sure. This piece of paper, in front of us on the screen now *(see opposite)* seems much like the intentionally blank page. It is an art work, albeit a modest one. At the bottom of the page you read 'after Joseph Kosuth, after Douglas Huebler, after Lawrence Weiner.., Artforum, Vol. 36, No. 3, 1997, page 16', the work's title as well as an acknowledgement of its pedigree and provenance. It was commissioned in 2003 by the curator Lars Bang Larsen for a project that invited the audience to participate by photocopying the artists' contributions, to bring out what was there. As they waited by the photocopier to see what comes out after all the writing in art magazines, the discoveries of the giants of conceptual art, and after my own feeble efforts, it may have crossed their minds that what was there was already present.

This, finally, is an intentionally not a blank page from my forthcoming book, *Conversation Guide* – here it is, as blank as a page as you can ever get. *(See overleaf)*

Pavel Büchler is an artist, teacher and occasional writer on art, film and political culture. A founder of the Cambridge Darkroom Gallery and former Head of Fine Art at the Glasgow School of Art, he is currently Research Professor in Art and Design at Manchester Metropolitan University. Recent publications include *Conversation Pieces* (i3, 2003) and *Saving the Image: Art after Film*, co-edited with Tanya Leighton. (CCA, 2003). He is participating in the Istanbul Biennale, September 2005.

THIS PAGE IS INTENTIONALLY BLANK

Discussion:
Pavel Büchler, Sally O'Reilly, Jane Rendell

Contributors *Rose Butler, Jessica Calow, Emma Cocker, Horatio Eastwood, Jaspar Joseph-Lester, Joanna Laromani, Miranda Laughlin, Patrick Meighan, Tom Newell, Nastassia Page, Natalie Smith, Nick Stewart, Penny Whitehead*

PW *Jane, would you say more about the relation between text and image in the work? When you were doing the readings, they were visual, yet you also showed images at the same time.*

JR In previous work the images have been used as illustrations in a conventional way, but here they play a different role. Recently I realized that the theoretical description is quite dry, and I wanted to provide listeners with a double position where they are able to escape into the space that the images open up. This could produce a difficult position for the audience in trying to do two things at once, but it is something that has now become my intention. It is important to me how the art work is revealed and I have played with this in a number of ways. Sometimes I don't show any images of art work; I write the image through the text, and then I show the image later. This works differently from showing an image and then describing it in words, or allowing the two to appear in parallel. At the moment this is work in progress. I'm interested in how text and image work together and how different meanings or interpretations are produced by the order and way in which visual material is shown.

JL *You use the terms 'in the middle' and 'around the edge', spaces that are not allocated. When you talk about architecture, you are interested in the places that are ignored or marginalized. How do these unusual places open up the space for new subjectivities?*

JR I'm interested in architectural specifications – a particular language used to describe detailing. Certain spatial metaphors like 'in the middle' or 'in the centre' might be traditional ways of thinking about how architectural space is occupied. But to describe being behind the skirting board, is to get a glimpse of what that space might be like from reading the architects' specification, how they thought it should be put together – this is a different way of occupying the space, one that uses the imagination. My work is about combining the positions of these two different languages. The architectural specification appears to be clear and objective but it appears that even the empirical, objective language of architectural specification is subjective. I chose to use specifications for the text for the LLAW project on the external wall of the bookartbookshop after noticing the subjective language of a friend who is an architect. In her specifications she used words like 'gently' and 'carefully', which you won't find used in books on how to write specifications. I started to think that it is the most objective language that might be the most subjective. Perhaps the particularity of positions, how materials relate to each other in the architectural detail, could speak to the questions that you are raising about political empowerment, but in a way that is implicit rather than explicit.

ML *This perhaps takes up the previous question – would you say more about the differences and links between memory and imagination?*

JR Remembering – or memories – can be used as imaginative positions. In using remembered scenes when I am writing art criticism (sometimes autobiographical pieces and sometimes more generic memories), I'm producing a different position from which to imagine the work, because the person who reads the work – or listens to it – doesn't have my history, they cannot possibly be remembering what I remember, so the only way to access this is through the imagination. I am using memory in order to create possibility. Although some of the work is nostalgic, looking back in some way, the intention is not to return to that supposed original moment but to see what can be produced out of it. One of the texts that really influenced me was by bell hooks, in which she writes that we never quite remember things as they were, so there is always a slippage. In this case there is also a blurring between remembering and creating. What is important to me is that memory is a productive act. I am not interested in whether I remember correctly, but in the act of recall itself.

Audience *Why did you translate the pieces into different languages?*

JR The texts were going to Korea and I wanted people to understand them in their own language. As a result of the translations (as so often happens with my work), what appears to be purely practical produces something unusual and unexpected. I left the decision about who should do the translations to someone else, who chose an older man to read the texts. To hear what I had written about my girlhood read in the voice of an older Korean man alienated me from my own writing in some way. It separated me from it, allowing me space to be more inventive. When the texts were translated back into English, they were not quite the same and that further slippage interested me.

Audience *Sally, I enjoyed your performance of* Implicasphere. *Do you think it could work as a performance rather than a publication?*

SO'R We'd like to work on it as a radio piece, because of the challenge of showing images on the radio. It reminds me of a Winalot advert that was once translated to radio: some guy saying 'Oh see that Labrador over there, look at his ears streaming in the wind', and that might be a rather interesting way of colliding language with images. As for presenting it as a performance, the perpetual reading is quite difficult and there's no room for improvisation in *Implicasphere* – that's what I found out today. It is a real problem, the sheer panic of realising that I have to read it all quickly and you have to take it in as well.

JJ-L *Would you keep the same order or does it change every time?*

SO'R It would change every time. Making an *Implicasphere* is an organic process.

NP *The issues of* Implicasphere *are predominantly about the process, the thought and research rather than communication through the broadsheet. Do you believe the format of the broadsheet can portray this process fully so readers might invent their own* Implicasphere?

SO'R That's precisely the idea. This static piece of paper is a false representation of our process. Hopefully the process continues once it is out in the world. Our process is delta-like in that it comes to a point, and then, because there are all the references under each section – where it came from, who wrote it – it points back into the world for people to follow, to find the whole from which the extract has been wrested.

NP *To return to the performative element of your presentation, is there also a performative element to the collection of information for* Implicasphere?

SO'R In a way – certainly there is an invitation to other people to take part. I'm not sure if it's performative but it is generative.

JJ-L *There remains an editing process of sorts. How do you go about that?*

SO'R *Implicasphere* is a representation of our own implicaspheres – the orbits of association that a single word, concept or image might ripple outwards. If someone says 'bread', you might think 'toast', if you have quite narrow implicaspheres. If you have quite wide ones, you might think 'raven'.

PB Or 'nose'.

SO'R Yes, someone with wide implicaspheres might say 'nose'. Narrow implicaspheres are representative of somebody not so imaginative; really wide, of somebody extremely imaginative and creative, or maybe mad, implicaspheres so wide that no one can understand the associations. The point of the broadsheet is that it is a portrait of our process. It denotes the way that we have travelled through the infinite sea of possible content.

Audience *What happens to meaning?*

SO'R It comes back to the theme of this series, inscription. Meaning is reciprocal. When you place two things next to one another, one casts a shadow of significance over the other. Meaning is turned into something active. You could say that we are evangelical in that we are lifting things out of their original context so that meaning is no longer fixed. Because you can't be sure that meaning that is attached to the producer's original intention, it could have ossified through continuous historical misinterpretations. What we do by isolating it from that context and placing it in a new one is that, rather than closing down meaning, we are opening it out through butting it next to things that it would never usually be allowed to be next to.

NSt *Isn't that just a definition of poetics?*

SO'R *Just* a definition of poetics! Oh, that's *just* poetics!

NSt *What's the difference between* Implicasphere *and collage?*

SO'R Very little, other than collage generates new meaning from a new visual parity. With *Implicasphere*, the elements have a more complex trail of meaning, because of the text content and the palpable cultural contexts that cling to it like an aura. The new context isn't overwhelming. It's not a new image that we've built in *Implicasphere*; it's more of a cloud.

JC *The way you collate the information for* Implicasphere *sounds utopian in that you take it from here, there and everywhere, from different disciplines. It defies traditional hierarchies around areas of academic knowledge. In doing that, are you creating new hierarchies?*

SO'R We can't create new hierarchies of knowledge or significance in a space as limited and as transitory as *Implicasphere*. What we can do is to question those hierarchies. We are exploding the linear way that academia travels.

EC *I like the way that you described it as a cloud, the way that you brought the material together with a possibility that it then would disperse. As a printed broadsheet, it has a temporary quality.*

SO'R Yes, the structure, the grid is delineated by dotted lines, which imply that it's a semi-permeable membrane that holds things apart and it might just explode outwards at any minute; it is very gaseous.

NSm *What editing processes do you use? How do you create the structure from such a broad range of material?*

SO'R We try to find a spread of different disciplines and ways of presenting image and text, combination of both, and tones of voice. In the performance it becomes flattened into my voice, but in the broadsheet there is the sarcastic, the comedic, and the deeply serious. The figurative use of the theme, i.e. string or mice, is important and has metaphorical ramifications. Some elements are more resonant than others.

Audience *Does your own implicasphere have implications for the project?*

SO'R We author it in the editing process.

RB *In the attempts to override linear editing, lifting information and isolating it from the historical, do you find it frustrating when you give presentations or when you create* Implicasphere, *that you're then pinning down what you've collected into a linear structure?*

SO'R In the performative version it does feel frustrating that it is linear, that it tumbles through time. With the paper version, the frustration is the edges of the piece of paper. It could be folded in half at least another seven times and we could still fill it, and the frustration is that we can't reflect the enormous plethora of stuff that we find. But that's nowhere near as frustrating as the linear. There are so many links that could be made between the nose elements that I'd need an enormous chalkboard to link them all.

EC *Pavel, I must have incredibly bad short-term concentration in terms of being overwritten by information. I'm obviously trying to think about what we're going to talk about but at the same time go off into different direction. What struck me particularly about your presentation was the page you showed, the phrase that read: 'This page is left intentionally blank'. When we come to these kinds of events, we're already overwritten by previous knowledge about a practice, the previous times when we've heard somebody speak. In the lecture you gave in* Transmission: Speaking & Listening, *'Responsibility' last year, you said an artist's responsibility is to make nothing happen. What is the connection between that blank page and the idea of the artist's responsibility to make nothing happen?*

PB In the abstract on what I was going to say and what in the end, I did not say, there is a reference *via* Howard Britton and Jacques Lacan to Martin Heidegger, who describes the production of a work of art like the making of a vase out of nothing, in such a way that the nothing that was there in the first place becomes the void that makes the vase what it is, the void inside the vase. That is quite a good metaphor for what artists do. There is something unarticulated in the world that needs to be articulated. So when I say that I want to make nothing happen, it is meant to be understood in the sense that articulated nothing becomes something active. So it is nothing as something. At the same time I believe that there is far too much art in the world already, and so it's better to take things easy.

EC *There's an interesting counter-position between* Implicasphere *and the idea of the artist striving for the blank page. There's an exciting tension in those two possibilities in relation to inscription.*

PM *You made it clear that it was something that occurs in the present, now that you've given it to us, the audience, through spoken words, we've placed it in our memories. We've written down what we've chosen to write down. In giving a presentation to an audience, have you made the presentation go away? Does asking the question make it come back again?*

PB I didn't make the present go away – I have nothing to do with the arrow of time, that's just how things are. I'm trying to do the opposite in a presentation – I'm trying to make the present moment last, to shape it in such a way that it may be remembered. It is an attempt not to just let things slip away but to mark a moment so it could be referred to.

TN *In the text-based work, you add in order to take away, and yet in the sound-based work, the LIVE album, you took away the music to add a different element. Did you consciously change your method of working in order to translate the ideas into sound?*

PB It occurred to me while I was listening to a 1970s improvised jazz live recording, that I was there, physically. It was an extraordinary feeling, to be physically present there on that piece of vinyl because I went to that concert. The music is beautiful, but the sense that I have left a trace on that album is more interesting, so I tried to devise a way of recovering that. Of course I add something, but I try to interfere as little as I can, partly because I'm lazy and partly because, as I said, it doesn't really take that much. The great lesson of modern art is how little it takes to make something ordinary, extraordinary. So there is no addition, it's simply rummaging through my record collection, bringing all these records together then getting rid of the aspect it is supposed to have, namely the music, and seeing what what is left looks like. Once you've done that, you realize that there are many other things that the work does as well. I got an invitation to do a show in Hanover at the Grammophonfabrik, the former Deutsche Grammophon factory. The gallery contacted Deutsche Grammophon to see if they might be interested as sponsors and the PR guys expressed some interest and continued talking, until one day I had a phone call from a humourless German lawyer in the legal department of Deutsche Grammophon who said no way would his company be associated with this project because it was piracy. I said 'Hold on a minute, if it is piracy I am only taking what's mine. Where are my royalties for clapping?' After a short discussion, the guy said 'The best thing I can do for you, sir, is to forget this conversation the moment I put the phone down.'

EC *In Howard Britton's essay on your work, 'How To Make It Go Away', his view on what 'it' is changes throughout the text. He suggests that you take the*

vase and dismantle it, taking the viewer into the void. The writing brings 'it'
back. Britton says that when meaning is incomplete, it sets the audience to
work in that it must be active, mediating between meaning and non-meaning.
What is the role of the critic, as it would seem he or she is putting the vase
back together, making 'it' come back?

PB   I call it intention; he calls it authorship. What you are trying to
make go away is the idea of – not a fixed meaning – a recommended
meaning. I do not believe that there is such a thing as fixed meaning
but there is the meaning that you are directed toward by convention,
by context, or some other means. Howard says that my technique
makes the reader into an interpreter, a constructor of meaning. The
metaphor of the broken and reconstructed, reconstituted vase is
beautiful, but for me it's simpler. I do not rely on the reader. Of
course there would be no art without audience, and it is the critical
reader who gives a work its meaning. But that's something that has to
be negotiated between the work and the critical reader, not between
the author and the critical reader. It's not that the work is merely the
mediating agency. It's more that the artist's powers do not extend that
far. No matter what you say that the work is, the work still is what it
is. No matter how often you tell me this page is intentionally blank, it
is not blank. So all that the artist can do is make the work potent with
intention or potent as a site. I don't think that you give the reader
fragments that can be put together; you give only an empty vase.
John Cage beautifully spoke of an empty glass and why the empty
glass needs to be empty in reference to his composition '4.33', which
as you all know is four minutes and thirty three seconds of silence.
He says the glass has to be empty so that if an idea comes along, we
have something to pour it into. The way I think about it is you have
the milk, you have the glass, the glass becomes a glass of milk – well,
does anyone really need a glass of milk? When we are thirsty we want
milk, not a glass of milk. A glass of milk is a thing that needs to be
dealt with, to be handled; something needs to be done with it to
release its potential. A glass of milk is a fixed thing; milk is what you
really want. A work of art is a fixed thing; art is what you really want.

JR   To return to the question about how the critic attempts to place
meaning, this is a role that some critics choose, but this isn't what
interests me in my work. Sally's phrase 'proximity inscribes meaning'
is key here; with the work that I'm doing, depending on the context,
people want to inscribe different meanings to the work of criticism.
If I'm on a panel with other critics, for example, they might want
my work to point to a more specific meaning in the work of Elina

Brotherus, say, whereas I want to resist that. I want to open up conversations and that can be difficult across criticism, writing and art. Sometimes it happens that the work can't be resolved. It's different for works of art to propose something that's unresolved, producing a cloud of association, than for criticism to do so. What happens when criticism refuses to define meaning?

Audience   *Is it still criticism then or is it a response?*

JR   That's a question that comes up frequently in interdisciplinary conversations, about whether a word or a term – art, architecture, theory, criticism – whether we are interested in expanding the term to hold more meaning, or whether we leave a specific meaning ascribed to that term and then, when we start to do something different, we move into a different field. I'm caught here because I'm interested in this expanded field of criticism, testing the edge of it, but I'm also interested in what happens when you might describe that as writing, when you work through analogy, and the possibilities are opened up. I'm interested in that two-way movement.

HE   *Going back to Emma's suggestion that Pavel's blank page is opposite to Sally's Implicasphere – with Implicasphere you start with something, like the nose, and you move through a free association, which would imply moving towards a hidden object, like a graph of desire, and in revealing more with each thread it seems to be hiding more of the meaning in the sense that you never actually deal specifically with the nose, what a nose actually is, what it means to be a nose. Then, Pavel, in revealing that 'this is a blank page', you are doing the opposite by hiding the page, so again desire enters. With your glass of milk, it would seem that all we really want is just to want.*

PB   Yes.

SO'R   He says 'yes', I say 'hmm'. I'm intrigued by your use of the word desire. I haven't applied desire to our implicaspherical process before. Our pathways aren't linear, they're radiating, so perhaps the desire is one of entropy, to be led every which way, and there isn't a process of revelation but of the blind being lead.

EC   *In the way that Jane was talking about the critic's response, and in connection to Pavel's work, I'm interested in the idea of burial, which has come up in some of the recent Transmission lectures. The act of burial serves different functions in that it is both protective and destructive. The way that you talked about it in relation to the diary entries was interesting in the sense that the overwriting buried the information at the heart of what you were saying. Criticism can sometimes bury the object, the work of art, in the protective shroud of other ideas or theory.*

JR   I wouldn't want to say 'bury'...

PB Neither would I...

JR I'm interested in what happens in the writing over and over again until the work becomes something different. There is the possibility in art criticism – and maybe this is what you were referring to – that if the work of art itself disappears because the critic is overwriting, then a serious problem emerges. I'm more interested in a process of association and how the critic's work could operate through association. Not burying – I would be worried if that were so.

PB I agree, it's not the best choice of word, but why would you be worried about reaching a point where the work disappear from sight? All it does is disappears from sight, it does not disappear. And if it does, so what? Why would you be worried about it?

JR Because what I'm really interested in is the relationship that I'm making with the work and also with the artist and there's an ethics to any project about dialogue. If my text was to bury the work, that wouldn't be an ethical dialogue. That would be my concern.

SO'R As a critic, I agree that there is the old idea of the critic applying meaning to something and in that sense there is a possibility of burial, but now it's a more interrogative process, about rooting around for different types of meaning that come from different points of inception. So there is the intentional meaning, the unintentional, the accidental, the associative meaning. As a critic, I feel that my job is to negotiate all of those and give them equal attention.

JR To bring to the surface that process in the same way that that process is surfaced in *Implicasphere*?

SO'R Yes, so that the writing is not just descriptive or illustrative but demonstrative of a process. The process of art writing or art criticism, in whatever guise, fits quite naturally within the artist's process of making the work. Writing about an artist isn't just writing about the object or the outcome, but also about the process.

JR What about the process you're involved in *Implicasphere*? There are the associative chains that are produced when you're gathering the information, and then there's a selection and an editing of the work on the page, and today something else happened around improvising the gaps. Do you think that any of those processes are more akin to your work as a critic? Are any of them similar to the way that you might operate when you write?

SO'R What is less similar is finding the whole nuggets, and placing them next to one another. It's much more generative.

JJ-L *There's also a sense in which the project is critical as a process. The notion of creating a generative series of associations makes me think about how you might criticize or disrupt an idea of fixed meaning. It's in the process that we find something critical.*

SO'R   Yes, demonstrative rather than illustrative of what Pavel is talking about, finding the intentional meaning and then subverting that through process and new context.

PB   The function of criticism is not just to identify the intention of the author or the intended meaning but also to question readings of the work. So the critic has to always triangulate, in respect of both of those sides.

JR   Also to make connections to the greater social set of relations surrounding those particular relations because otherwise the operation is too internal, and only revolves around the relation between the critic, the work and the artist. It is important to keep in mind how that conversation relates to social and political questions.

Reading List

Provenance

Nicholas Bourriaud, *Postproduction*, London: Art Data 2003.
Nicholas Bourriaud, *Relational Aesthetics*, Dijon: Les Presses de réel 2002.
Douglas Crimp, *On the Museum's Ruins*, Cambridge, Mass: MIT 1995.
Neil Cummings and Marysia Lewandowska, *The Value of Things*,
    London/Basel: August/Birkjauser 2000.
Robertson Davis, *The Cornish Trilogy*, Harmondsworth: Penguin 2003.
Thierry du Duve, *Kant after Duchamp*, Cambridge, Mass: MIT 1996.
Michel Foucault, *The Order of Things*, London: Routledge 2001.
J.K. Huysmans, *Against Nature (A rebours)*, Harmondsworth: Penguin 2003.
Joseph Kosuth, *Art after Philosophy and After, Collected Writings*,
    Cambridge, Mass: MIT 1991.
Marcel Mauss, *The Gift*, London: Routledge 1990.

Film/documentary:
The Rebel, featuring Tony Hancock, directed by Robert Day,
    written by Alan Simpson & Ray Galton (105 mins) 1960.
Tate Modern 3: *The Enemy Within*, featuring Jake Chapman and
    Marcel Duchamp, directed by Simon Chu (60 mins) 2000.

Inscription

Victor Burgin, *The Remembered Film*, London: Reaktion 2004.
Jacques Derrida, *Writing and Difference*, trans. Alan Bass,
    Chicago: Chicago University Press 1978.
Johanna Drucker, *The Alphabetic Labyrinth; The Letters in History and Imagination*,
    London: Thames & Hudson 1995.
Alberto Manguel, *A History of Reading*, London: Flamingo 1997.
W. J. T. Mitchell, *Picture Theory, Essays on Verbal and Visual Representation*,
    Chicago: University of Chicago Press 1995.
Michael Newman, Jon Bird (eds), *Rewriting Conceptual Art*, London: Reaktion 1999.

Acknowledgements

As ever, many people have contributed to *Transmission: Speaking & Listening* in many ways. We would like to thank the following: for technical assistance and organisation, the staff of the Showroom, Tom Figures, Jessie Itofo, Richard Moore, Mark Todd, David Winstanley and especially, Richard Bolam; for support from Site Gallery, Rowena Hamilton, Matthew Jarvis and George Rogers; for transcribing the discussions (and getting them to the editors on time), Natalie Allistone, Richard Arber, Jennifer Ash, Silvia Brandstetter, Jessica Calow, Allie Carr, Rebecca Connolly, Jessamie Self, Leah Southwell-Wright, Claire Sterland, Penny Whitehead; and Katie Davies for her patience in transferring recordings of the lectures and discussions to CD.

We are grateful to our colleagues in Fine Art at Sheffield Hallam University, who continue to support the lecture series and publication, with their presence at lectures, their contributions to discussions and with their generosity of creative thinking. We owe particular thanks to Professor Chris Rust and the Art and Design Research Committee; and also to Meg Handscombe for helping us balance our books. We also thank Carol Maund and Jeanine Griffin at Site Gallery.

Our copy editor John X. Berger continues his sterling work, as do Ben Weaver and Patrick Ward in designing this series. As Volume 4 is completed and added to the previous volumes on the bookshelf, the compulsion to run one's hand over them increases, and while as editors we tend to see what we have omitted or failed to correct, there is also the secret yield of pride and pleasure.

Transmission; Speaking & Listening exists only because of the exchange that is possible in the productive encounter of artist, writer and audience. At times the exchange is immediate, even passionate; at other times it develops slowly, over weeks or months, and one returns to what was said in the reconstruction of memory, as much as in the reading of a book. Transmission is also an internalized act, and so we acknowledge those who do not speak as much as those who do, for they are not recorded here.

Also still available:

Transmission: Speaking & Listening Volume 1
(September 2002)
'Spatiality, Homelessness and Anxiety' and 'Performativity, Repetition and Acting-out'
Contributors: Jane Rendell, Sophy Rickett, Rut Blees Luxemburg, Cornford & Cross,
Laura Godfrey-Isaacs, Vong Phaophanit, Andrew Grassie, Dutton & Peacock, Mary Evans, Breda Beban,
Roxy Walsh, Sharon Kivland, Duncan McLaren, Jane Prophet, Alan Johnston, Noble & Silver,
Kristin Mojsiewicz, Sonia Boyce, Neal Beggs, Adam Chodzko, Simon Patterson, Daniel Marquez,
Susan Johanknecht, Laura Horelli

Transmission: Speaking & Listening Volume 2
(September 2003)
'The Surface of the Image' and 'The Impulse of Narrative'
Contributors: Darian Leader, Sarah Wigglesworth, Mark Fairnington, DJ Simpson, Mariele Neudecker,
Sophie Benson, Grayson Perry, Claude Heath, Joan Key, Michael Archer, Chlöe Brown, Erin Mouré,
Mark Aerial Waller, Tom Hunter, Zineb Sedira, Daniel Sturgis, Jacques Nimki, Frances Hegarty,
Alice Maude-Roxby, Clémentine Deliss

Transmission: Speaking & Listening Volume 3
(September 2004)
'Ornament and Utility' and 'Responsibility'
Contributors: Jeanne Randolph, Sarah Staton, Mikey Cuddihy, Dan Hays, George Shaw, David Mabb,
Kate Blacker, Simon Periton, David Thorp, Monika Oechsler, Pavel Büchler, Paul Rooney,
Conroy/Sanderson, Eggebert-and-Gould, Jananne Al-ani, Jemima Stehli, David Bate, Kathrin Böhm

Forthcoming in September 2006:

Transmission: Speaking & Listening Volume 5
'Daily Encounters'